SPACE AND GRACE
TO BUILD
A BIGGER AND BETTER MARRIAGE

Stephen Hall
and Vanessa Hall

SPACE AND GRACE
TO BUILD A BIGGER AND BETTER MARRIAGE

ISBN: 9780692722367

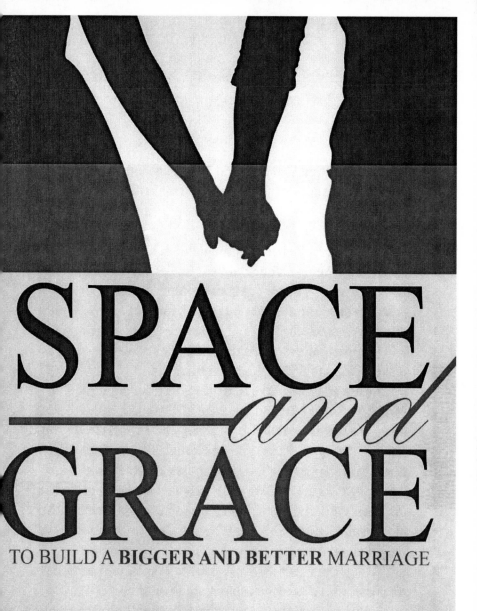

SPACE *and* GRACE

TO BUILD A **BIGGER AND BETTER** MARRIAGE

STEPHEN & VANESSA HALL

FOREWORD BY JOSEPH W. WALKER, III

Acknowledgements

First, we want to thank God for his unconditional love toward us. We appreciate the many persons who walked with us through this reflective journey: our parents, Pastor Edward and Anna Hall and James and Bertha Morris, whose prayers and love undergirded us all throughout our lives. (We will never forget you!) We thank our children, Ember, Stephen II, and Anthony; and we thank our grandchildren. (Thanks for the great Sunday brunches that we so look forward to.) We would also like to thank the Hall and Morris families for their unwavering support, especially our niece Kaye Gibson, who helps make it easy to fulfill God's will for our lives.

We are grateful for the leadership of Presiding Bishop Joseph W. Walker, III and Dr. Stephaine Walker; Bishop Paul S. Morton and Pastor Debra B. Morton; and our pastor, Bishop James H. Morton, whose love and leadership have been priceless. Thanks to the Full Gospel Baptist Church Fellowship, especially the state of Georgia, which we were privileged to lead for seven years and is now led by Bishop Lionel Catchings. We also thank God for the Rhema Nation Church, which we have the privilege to serve joyfully.

To all of our friends, thank you for your caring heart and for every word that made a difference in our lives.

We give special thanks to Johnny Stephens and Grassroots Publishing. Thanks also to Dr. Kathy Armistead, Dr. Brian Keith Hodges, Dr. Craig Oliver, Dr. Kerwin Lee, and Dr. Tolan Morgan for your phenomenal contributions and support.

May the rest of your days be the best of your days!

TABLE OF CONTENTS

Foreword

This book is full of wisdom and advice from a respected Christian couple. There's a lot more to marriage than saying "I do." It is a commitment made by two people before God. In general, we all know what marriage is, but this book takes us a step further.

Authors Bishop Stephen Hall and Vanessa Hall also say that bigger and better marriages can happen only because of our bigger and better faith in God. It's God who is our Maker and Creator. As 1 John 4:19 (NIV) says, "We love because he first loved us." We are able to give each other the gifts of space and grace because God gives them to us first. God intends for us to position ourselves for success in our marriages by first looking to Him.

This book will inform and inspire you. It will help you not only to be more faithful believers but also to be able to give a more authentic witness as a couple, even during times of stress and heartache. Every marriage shifts over time, and resets are necessary, but trouble and temptations can make you stronger. What people mean for evil, God can intend for your good.

Too many books only tell you what you should do or what you need to do. This book is packed with examples and will teach you how to do.

In your marriage you have a choice: You can choose to make your marriage bigger and better, or you can choose to have a marriage that lacks purpose and fails to fulfill its destiny. This book takes seriously the conviction that your freedom to choose is based on your desire to live by God's principles as expressed in His Word.

I am indebted to Bishop Stephen Hall and Vanessa Hall for taking on this important project. Through their work, they will show you how a bigger and better marriage looks.

Bishop Joseph W. Walker, III
Senior Pastor, Mount Zion Church Nashville TN
Presiding Bishop of Full Gospel Baptist International Fellowship

Introduction

Who doesn't want a bigger and better marriage? If you're not married yet, a bigger and better marriage is probably something you dream about. We all want to be better. We want a bigger and better faith, better relationships and families, better careers, and bigger and better finances.

When we position ourselves to be bigger and better, we stand tall. We are open about where we stand and what we stand for; but if there is one area in our lives where we need to be bigger and better, it's in our marriages. A bigger and better marriage is one that will stand the test of time, one that is strong enough to prevail through the storms and trials of life, and one we can count on when all else fails.

"That's nice," you may say, "but how do we get a bigger and better marriage?" More than half of all marriages—even Christian marriages—fail, so is having a bigger and better marriage only a wish? In a word—no.

Bigger and better. That's how Vanessa and I think about our marriage. Our marriage is built upon The Biggest and The Best—God—who is our ultimate Strength and Redeemer. You can have a bigger and better marriage, too, but having such a marriage isn't guaranteed.

Having a successful marriage takes intentionality and perseverance. It takes time and practice. It takes a mutual willingness for you and your spouse to share your space—your mental, emotional, and physical space. It also takes grace because none of us are perfect. Sharing space and offering grace are key to building a successful marriage, the kind of marriage God wants you to have.

> *He answered and said unto them, Have ye not read, that he which made them at the beginning made them male and female,*
>
> *And said, for this cause shall a man leave father and mother, and shall cleave to his wife: and they twain shall be one flesh?*
>
> *Wherefore they are no more twain, but one flesh. What therefore God hath joined together, let not man put asunder. (Matthew 19:4-6, KJV)*

Do not think this book is meant to make you "holier than thou." It is not meant to call down judgment on you or for you to use it to criticize others. We're not talking about a spiritualized view of marriage or a fairytale marriage.

God lives outside church walls just like we do, and he has everything to do with real life. Church is his place of repose; it's where we worship him. The world, however, is where you and I live most of the time, and it's where we can work with God to achieve his purposes.

We may come to church, volunteer for the church, and do mission and reach the lost on behalf of the church, but we live at home. At church we may celebrate marriage and go to marriage workshops, but at home is where we work on our marriages. However, it is also true that couples and families that go to church together have a far better chance of having successful marriages and staying together than those who don't.

A Bigger and Better Marriage Is a Gift From God

Marriage is a gift from God, but like any divine gift, it must be nurtured and cared for. It must be protected and provided for. Such a gift may call us to change, adapt, and position ourselves differently, but God's gifts are always for our benefit. The rewards are well worth the risks because receiving a gift from God is risky business, and he will always give us things that will stretch us and help us grow into the people he intends for us to be.

Yes, God is intentional about what he gives and to whom he gives it, and he never gives us a gift without us having to reach out to receive it. The gifts God gives are meant to be used to create a better life and a better world. They are never meant to be horded or hidden under a bushel. No, God's gifts are meant to be shared openly.

That's what Vanessa and I are doing in this book. We are sharing from our hearts and our experiences.

Over the years, we have built a bigger and better marriage, and we want to help you build one, too. Your marriage won't look exactly like ours. You are different people, after all, and we all will embody the principles of a solid marriage differently.

What is great for us may not be your cup of tea. What you believe is wonderful might not work in our situation. However, as Christians, we share a faith in a God who promises to clear a path for us, to stand with us, and to support us in our times of need. We all can share sound biblical principles that will help us navigate tough times and unforeseen obstacles.

A Bigger and Better Marriage Is Intentional

God is intentional, and he wants us to intentionally build our homes and our marriages on his sure foundation. If we are ever going to reach the mountaintop of a marriage full of space and grace, we have to start with God's plan, or else we'll never make it.

With God as our foundation, we can build with confidence, and we will succeed. A house is only as good as its foundation. It doesn't matter if a building is made of the most expensive materials, if the foundation is faulty, the house will collapse.

A few years ago, a building collapsed in St. Charles, Illinois. According to the head of the city building and zoning commission, one of the building's foundation walls failed, causing the second story to drop about eighteen inches, dooming the entire structure.

All buildings have to have structural integrity, which means that they are built to withstand a load, including their own weight, in order to resist breaking or bending. Integrity is intentional, and it assures that the construction will perform its designed function, during reasonable use, for as long as the designed life of the structure. Solid homes, like all buildings, are thoughtfully constructed with intentionality to ensure that catastrophic failure does not occur. Such failure could result in injury, severe damage, monetary loss, and/or death.

In much the same way, bigger and better marriages are intentionally designed to withstand the inevitable storms of life and to last a lifetime. They are constructed to protect you from catastrophic failure, injury, monetary loss, and perhaps even an untimely death. Just like a building, a marriage takes time, skill, and commitment to see it through, even when times are tough.

Being intentional is especially important for couples as they step into new things. That's what Stephen and I discovered when we realized my life-long dream to publish a Christian magazine. I had always wanted to build a magazine that shows women how God wants us to be all we can be. To some of you "being all you can be" may sound trite, but for me, living by godly standards of excellence is vitally important, because they represent foundational truths for all successful relationships.

Yes, publishing *Elect Lady Magazine* is my dream, and Stephen has been there with me every step of the way. But new endeavors, no matter how exciting or promising, can also be challenging for a marriage. We're all creatures of habit, and starting a new adventure means that some of those old habits may not survive and probably don't need to survive if they threaten to get in the way. In our case, starting a new business meant that our roles in the family would have to be more flexible and perhaps shift.

Almost immediately, I realized that I couldn't do all I wanted to do for my family, at least not like I'd done it before. In the past, my time and energy were focused primarily on building a healthy home for our family. My husband and family had been my priorities, but now the magazine competed for my attention. That meant that Stephen had to make adjustments, too. He could no longer just assume that I'd be available to cook dinner or run one of the kids somewhere or that I'd be able to meet with a church committee any time. But rather than becoming frustrated and demanding, Stephen gave me space and grace.

I'm not saying that these changes were easy, because they weren't. Spending less time together is not a good idea if you want your marriage to thrive, but having less time and competing priorities also meant that the time we did have together became more precious. And we've had to become more intentional about planning for our "together time," because if we're not intentional, we needlessly waste our opportunities for sharing our love with each other.

As the magazine continues to take off, my self-confidence has soared, and my confidence in our marriage has gone through the roof. I am so grateful for Stephen's support. It's exciting to see him excited about my dream coming true. When Stephen says that he's my number one cheerleader, it makes me love him even more and work harder to achieve what I believe God has planted in my heart to accomplish.

My husband's support empowers and encourages me. It makes me feel that I can do anything and that I was foolish to be afraid to step outside of the box that I'd built for myself, the box that had restricted my vision and held me captive. With the space and grace that Stephen offers and the joy I experience in realizing my dream, I have also found that my capacity to juggle priorities has also increased. I have more energy to keep my commitments and promises to my husband, family, and church. Because I'm experiencing joy in fulfilling my dream, I'm better able to extend to Stephen the space and grace he needs, so together we have built a bigger and better marriage.

Bigger and Better Marriages Are Not Fairytales

Bigger and better marriages are not fairytales. A couple doesn't build a solid, successful marriage by just wishing it will happen. Some marriages, even with the best intentions and commitment, will not make it, which is a sad and tragic fact.

Perhaps that is your situation. Maybe you've been hurt, or maybe you were the one who caused the marriage to fail. Perhaps you are thinking about marriage for the first time. Whatever your circumstance, this book will help you set your sights high and move on.

Unfortunately, some marriages will fail. These relationships are unhealthy and are making one or both of you sick—sick and tired or just sick and tired of being sick and tired. If you are or have been in an abusive relationship or in a marriage with someone who habitually lies or cheats, someone you can't trust, maybe it's time to get out.

This book is not going to say that everyone has to be married or that everyone's marriage will succeed beyond his or her wildest dreams. That's not reality. However, this book can help you negotiate some things that most likely will happen in your marriage—turning points, shifts, earthquakes, rock slides—that if not dealt with prayerfully, intentionally, and forthrightly can add enough stress to cause any marriage to collapse.

Bigger and Better Marriages Are About Family

Marriage and family go together. Even if a couple doesn't have children of their own, family is important. For one thing, each member of a couple brings into a marriage his or her own family history, with certain traditions and ways of doing things.

For example, in one wife's family of origin, her father took out the trash, and her mother oversaw the cooking but didn't necessarily do all of it. When the family sat down for dinner, they all sat together around the table, and one of the children offered a prayer before anyone ate anything.

In the husband's family, however, things were a bit different. Taking out the trash was a chore done by the children instead of the father. There were no regularly scheduled meals. Instead, everyone just grabbed something out of the refrigerator and found somewhere to eat, usually in front of the TV or the computer.

You may think that these are trivial things that don't matter. On the contrary, marriages can fail for smaller reasons than these. The point is that each person brings his or her history into a marriage, and that history includes the family of origin.

These days, I'm not sure that anyone can even define what a family is. Families come in all configurations: nuclear (parents and children), blended (step-parents and step-children), extended (multigenerational), couples (no children and maybe no pets, either), empty-nesters (grown-up children who live elsewhere).

Then there are combinations galore. Perhaps one partner has a child or children from a previous relationship; or perhaps the couple has lived together, has a couple of children, and is just now getting married. Perhaps the grandparents are raising the grandchildren. Perhaps the couple has foster children. Maybe the couple wants to adopt. The possibilities are endless.

While family configurations bring added stress to a marriage, this book is only about married couples or those who are considering marriage. Who knows? Maybe there'll be a later book about building bigger and better families. For the time being, while we acknowledge that families are important, that's not the focus of this book.

Bigger and Better Marriages Need Space

Marriage, as we talk about in this book, is a gift from God, one that we can receive with matchless joy. Your spouse is a gift from God. Your spouse deserves your honor and respect.

In order to be your life-partner, your spouse needs you—not your stuff, not your excuses, not your ambivalence—all of you. Don't get the wrong idea, though. Marriage doesn't mean you will be swallowed up by your partner. In other words, you don't disappear. A couple consists of two distinct people who intentionally choose to become one at particular times.

Being a married couple does not obliterate the two individuals who make the couple. When you get married your identity isn't destroyed. You may have shared hopes and dreams, but that doesn't eliminate your individual goals and ambitions. You still have those.

However, as a committed couple, your individual wants and needs are woven together into a beautiful fabric that is enriched by each person, and that is impossible without the contributions of both people. This means that you take the other person's values, beliefs, and even quirks into thoughtful consideration.

When we say that in marriage you keep your identity, it doesn't mean that you live like you are single "with benefits." Instead, it means that you may have to change.

On the one hand, there may not be space in your relationship for bowling every Saturday night. There may not be room in your shared budget for the latest computer or iPhone. On the other hand, however, there may be space for learning to enjoy new sports or interests where you can make space for just the two of you such as riding bikes or cooking together.

In our home, Vanessa and I recognize the need for space. Don't get me wrong. We love each other, but sometimes we just have to be alone.

Space Absorbs Marriage Bumps and Jolts

Think about space as the breathing room of a relationship. Or consider this: When you move, you pack a lot of boxes. If you are packing something breakable such as a lamp, you pack it in bubble wrap. The padding of the bubble wrap absorbs any bumps or jolts when the moving truck hits a pothole in the road.

That's what I mean when I talk about space. Space isn't there to keep you apart or to keep you from getting close. It's a way to absorb the occasional shocks and earthquakes any marriage goes through.

Space Is Breathing Room

Space also has another function. Every one of us has a preferred amount of personal space, including physical space. Have you noticed that some people like to be physically close, while others need more physical space between them? Some people hug everybody. Some people don't hug anybody.

Psychologists say that the degree of personal space a person needs is not just personal preference. It is also cultural. If you've traveled outside the United States, you've probably seen this difference.

As a group, Hispanics and Italians stand closer to others when they're interacting than, say, Northern Europeans. In some cultures, it's OK—in fact, it's encouraged—to touch the person with whom you are politely conversing. In other cultures, touching a stranger is strictly forbidden.

We all need personal space. It's our breathing room, and usually it extends out about an arm's length in distance. Get much closer, and watch the person you're approaching begin to feel uncomfortable. If you get too close, that person will move back. I've seen it hundreds of times at church after worship.

Betty, who likes to be close, is talking with Teddy, who doesn't like to be close to other people. It doesn't take long before Betty has Teddy backing up across the room, because every time Betty moves in to get closer, Teddy feels uneasy and backs up until there is nowhere left to go.

Physical space is important, yes, but we also need emotional space. If you're in a helping profession or have needed counseling, perhaps you'll know what I'm talking about.

Over the years, I've become more aware of people's need for emotional space. As a pastor, people come to me for counsel. They come to talk, but sometimes what they really want is to unload their feelings on me. They want to get rid of their anxieties, troubles, and heartache. This is normal because as human beings we have a need to share our feelings with someone.

Part of being a pastor is being the person with whom others share their emotional burdens; and as I listen to what's going on in their world, somehow I let them into my world. This is what offering empathy and listening to another person means. Another person feels heard only if you open up yourself, but this also means that it takes an emotional toll on the listener to hear the pain and sorrow that the person inevitably needs counsel about.

That's OK in small doses. Helping professionals have to maintain some space or objectivity between themselves and the person being listened to, but some people are so needy or are hurting so badly that they drain their counsellors emotionally. When that happens, these listening professionals need time and space to recover and regroup.

Perhaps you've experienced this as well. Are there people you've met or who are in your life who just wear you out? They are so needy or depressed that it seems as if they are sapping your strength or sucking you dry.

We only have so much to give. We only have so much emotional space for helping. That's why people get compassion fatigue. Compassion fatigue happens because helpers get drained. Their juices run dry. They are depleted. During those times, we have to fill our emotional tanks again so we can be effective in helping the next person who comes to us.

In marriage, you can't invade your spouse's personal space so much or so often that he or she becomes so depleted that he or she feels constantly drained dry. You need to back off sometimes or else you will be like Betty and Teddy, dancing across the floor until your spouse has his or her back against the wall.

Space is that breathing room you give each other. It gives you the room to be who you are, and it will bring fresh air into your relationship.

Grace Is Unearned

As space is an essential ingredient, so is grace. Grace is that ease we find in our marriage relationships. It is part of the GMC (grace, mercy, compassion) triad. Grace is the recognition that one spouse is not going to do what the other spouse wants all the time and that neither spouse is perfect.

Grace involves forgiveness. When we talk about God's grace for us, we say that grace is unearned, unmerited favor. God's grace is always freely given with no strings attached. The grace you offer your marriage partner is a reflection of God's grace. You give it because you love your partner.

You may have wondered when we were going to get to love. Yes, you need love, but so many of us have a warped picture of what love is. In the King James Version of the Bible, the word used for "love" is *charity*, but it illustrates what loving someone means.

Though I speak with the tongues of men and of angels, and have not charity, I am become as sounding brass, or a tinkling cymbal.

And though I have the gift of prophecy, and understand all mysteries, and all knowledge; and though I have all faith, so that I could remove mountains, and have not charity, I am nothing.

And though I bestow all my goods to feed the poor, and though I give my body to be burned, and have not charity, it profiteth me nothing.

Charity suffereth long, and is kind; charity envieth not; charity vaunteth not itself, is not puffed up,

Doth not behave itself unseemly, seeketh not her own, is not easily provoked, thinketh no evil;

Rejoiceth not in iniquity, but rejoiceth in the truth;

Beareth all things, believeth all things, hopeth all things, endureth all things.

Charity never faileth: but whether there be prophecies, they shall fail; whether there be tongues, they shall cease; whether there be knowledge, it shall vanish away.

For we know in part, and we prophesy in part.

But when that which is perfect is come, then that which is in part shall be done away.

When I was a child, I spake as a child, I understood as a child, I thought as a child: but when I became a man, I put away childish things.

For now we see through a glass, darkly; but then face to face: now I know in part; but then shall I know even as also I am known.

And now abideth faith, hope, charity, these three; but the greatest of these is charity. (1 Corinthians 13)

Perhaps you have or will use 1 Corinthians 13 at your wedding. Many couples have used this passage because it gives us a clear picture of what love is and is not. Love is unselfish and puts the other person's well-being before our own. God's love has no limits, but we are human, and our love does have limits.

Jesus also tells us to love our neighbor as ourselves. This means that we need to love ourselves and give ourselves grace, too. We need to cut ourselves some slack and be patient and kind to ourselves.

Loving your partner does not mean that you destroy yourself in the process, and it also does not mean that you love the other so much that you do everything for them. Love is not slavery. Love comes best from healthy individuals who are grounded in faith and self-knowledge.

Grace, like love, is always freely given. It's not like being forced to hug Aunt Nellie when you were little. Love is offered, and it should never be taken for granted. However, all of us have grown up with warped images of love to some degree because we all had human, therefore, imperfect parents.

Ultimately, grace comes from God, and we extend grace because we love our partner, which is also one way in which God loves us. He loved you enough to give you your partner. God loves your partner enough to give you to this relationship. "We love because he first loved us" (1 John 4:19, KJV). Love means that we recognize that sometimes our partner needs space.

Sometimes we need space, too, so we extend the grace for there to be space. Like love, grace is offered as a gift, and it should be received in that same spirit. It cannot be stolen, forced, or presumed; and it's given with no strings attached.

How to Use This Book

In this book we are going to look at marriage as a six-step journey.

- Every marriage begins with a first date.

- The dating period is followed by a commitment to be exclusive in the relationship.

- Then comes the prelude to marriage: premarital counseling and the honeymoon.

- At some point, children come into the picture.

- After the children grow up and are on their own, you and your partner become empty-nesters.

- Then you arrive at your golden years. If things go as they often do, you become grandparents and maybe great-grandparents.

However, each of these six steps also represents a shift in your relationship that must be intentionally managed.

In fact, these shifts are often jolts to a couple's relationship from which it may be hard to recover. In other words, things just don't naturally fall into place. The transition between each step can put your marriage in peril. Between each step there is rocky terrain that must be trod carefully if you plan to move up to the next one.

Vanessa and I want to tell you that at the end of the road, after you've climbed all six steps, you'll be on a mountaintop where you'll be able to look back over your life with gratitude, satisfaction, and a deep feeling of accomplishment.

We've made each of these steps into a chapter so you can see in greater detail what marriage looks like at each point. You'll find practical suggestions and what we call deal-breakers. However, throughout this book, Vanessa and I will show you how we are negotiating and traveling our God-ordained path. We're a long way from being finished, but we have built a strong marriage using these principles; and despite setbacks, we've made it this far together.

In this book you'll also find examples from couples with whom I've counseled over the years. However, as is customary in books like this, all identifying details of persons and situations have been changed to protect their privacy, and at no time have any confidences been broken.

Conclusion

As we travel the path God lays before us, we have to climb up the mountain to reach our goals; but like going on any adventure, we must first prepare. We have to have a map and a guide. That is what this book is intended to be: a map with a couple who's been there to help along the way. Vanessa and I have a wealth of experience, and we can help you avoid some of the hardships that inevitably will happen.

We all want to have bigger and better marriages, and we want to end up on the mountaintop of life basking in God's eternal glory. At the end of it all, we want to hear God say, "Well done, good and faithful servant."

CHAPTER ONE

DATING FOR A BIGGER AND BETTER MARRIAGE

Many claim to have unfailing love, but a faithful person who can find?

The righteous lead blameless lives; blessed are their children after them.

—Proverbs 20:6-7, NIV

DATING FOR A BIGGER AND BETTER MARRIAGE

What's on Your List?

I know a woman who when she was ten years old made a list of characteristics she wanted her husband to have. I, on the other hand, was a late bloomer.

However, after that failure, I did come up with a list of characteristics my future wife would have. She would be kind, intelligent, understanding of me and of my occupation, and able to express what she needs from me. She would have a desire for a fruitful sexual relationship, and she would be fun-loving and open to trying new things.

While I've matured and grown up, when I look at my wife now, I believe I was pretty successful in getting a woman with the qualities I had on my list. The point is that I was intentional about who I was looking for in a marriage partner. While not every person I dated matched up well with the qualities on my list, what I wanted was always in the back of my mind.

Pop psychology tells us that men are always on the hunt for a beautiful, sexy mate, but they aren't necessarily looking for a long-term relationship. We're told that men are always looking for and thinking about sex—and there is some truth to that.

Men typically think about sex a lot, but it's not true that men are only hunters and providers. A man's role is a lot more than hunting for food during the day and guarding camp from wild animals at night. In our culture, we've gotten a little carried away with this line of thinking and have underestimated what a real man can do.

Your best chance for a bigger and better marriage is to date people who conform to who God intends you to be.

Pop psychology also tells us that a man chases a woman until she lets him catch her and that a woman carefully bates a trap and pounces when a man enters the lair. We're also told that women make the best nurturers and caretakers.

Because of this cultural stereotype, even today some women believe they are like Sleeping Beauty, waiting for their true love, their Prince Charming, to rescue them. However, these cultural fictions are only half-truths at best. We all know wonderful, strong women who do not fit this mold.

Dating to build a bigger and better marriage begins with two people, a man and a woman. Your best chance to succeed in marriage is only to date people who conform reasonably well to who God intends you to be in the first place. So before we launch into a discussion of dating, we need to have a clear picture of the landscape of who to choose.

God's View of Manhood

The Bible tells us that God's view of who a man should be is fundamentally and foremost a person who has a right relationship with God. In Genesis, we read that God created humanity, mankind, in his own image.

First, a man is a child of God. He was created out of God's intent to have creatures who could love him back. We are made in God's image, men and women alike; but when we look in a mirror and see an image, that image can only do what we can do.

If you make a face in the mirror, the image in the mirror makes an identical face back at you. There is no variation. When you turn and walk away, so does the mirror image. When you're not there, the image is gone as well. The mirror image has no choice but to do what you do. In fact, you would think it was strange to say that the image in the mirror was real or could love you at all.

God works differently. We are a mirror reflection of God, but don't presume to think that we reflect all of who God is. We reflect only a tiny part. God is much greater than our imagining. Unlike our mirror image, we are free to reflect God or not to reflect him. God gives us that choice. However, when we choose not to reflect God, we take our eyes off of him and move away from him. That's what sin is, and it's where evil can enter into our lives.

When we choose to reflect God, we are in a right relationship with him. The Bible calls this "righteousness." Also, unlike the image that stares back at us in our mirrors, as images of God, we are free to love or not to love God in return.

Knowing our place in relation to God instills in us certain values, attitudes, and behaviors. We seek to know more about God; we seek wisdom. To turn away is utter foolishness. That's why in the Bible one of the gravest insults is to call someone a fool. We honor God in our thoughts and actions by doing what he requires, which is to "do justly, and to love mercy, and to walk humbly" (Micah 6:8, KJV).

Our relationship with God and our behavior toward him and others is the prime directive. This is not only for men. It's for everyone; it's all inclusive. Jesus says it this way: "Love the Lord thy God with all thy heart, and with all thy soul, and with all thy mind. This is the first and Great Commandment" (Matthew 22:37; also Deuteronomy 6:5, KJV).

Second—and this also applies to women—we are to love God with our whole being and "love [our] neighbor as [ourselves]. On these two commandments hang all the law and the prophets" (Matthew 22:40, KJV). This comes directly from Jesus, so there can be no doubt about what God wants.

These two commandments to love God first and to love our neighbors as ourselves frame everything else. They represent what is called the tenor of Scripture. They determine how we understand everything else.

I want to deal with something up front that may be somewhat of a touchy subject for many people—women in particular—because this Scripture has been used for years to keep women in a one-down position.

Submitting yourselves one to another in the fear of God.

Wives, submit yourselves unto your own husbands, as unto the Lord.

For the husband is the head of the wife, even as Christ is the head of the church: and he is the savior of the body.

Therefore as the church is subject unto Christ, so let the wives be to their own husbands in everything.

Husbands, love your wives, even as Christ also loved the church, and gave himself for it;

That he might sanctify and cleanse it with the

washing of water by the word,

That he might present it to himself a glorious church, not having spot, or wrinkle, or any such thing; but that it should be holy and without blemish.

So ought men to love their wives as their own bodies. He that loveth his wife loveth himself.

For no man ever yet hated his own flesh; but nourisheth and cherisheth it, even as the Lord the church:

For we are members of his body, of his flesh, and of his bones. (Ephesians 5:21-30, KJV)

Please reread the first sentence. A relationship between a man and a woman is mutually submissive. This may come as a surprise, but women aren't the only ones who submit. A husband and a wife submit to each other.

Does this mean men and women are the same? No. Does it mean men and women should play the same roles in the family? No. It does mean that when we love God first and love ourselves and our spouses second, we love each other as God intends.

In premarriage counseling or if a dating couple comes to me and the subject comes up, I point out that the husband is to love his wife as Christ loved the church, meaning that he laid down his life for her. Telling a couple this always makes for an interesting conversation, as it does in any mixed group at church or elsewhere.

Third, lest the latter part of Ephesians 5 only gets attention, the first part tells us that to be righteous, men and women should control their appetites.

Be ye therefore followers of God, as dear children;

And walk in love, as Christ also hath loved us, and hath given himself for us an offering and a sacrifice to God for a sweet-smelling savor.

But fornication, and all uncleanness, or covetousness, let it not be once named among you, as becometh saints;

Neither filthiness, nor foolish talking, nor jesting, which are not convenient: but rather giving of thanks.

For this ye know, that no whoremonger, nor unclean person, nor covetous man, who is an idolater, hath any inheritance in the kingdom of Christ and of God.

Let no man deceive you with vain words: for because of these things cometh the wrath of God upon the children of disobedience.

Be not ye therefore partakers with them.

For ye were sometimes darkness, but now are ye light

in the Lord: walk as children of light:

(For the fruit of the Spirit is in all goodness and righteousness and truth;)

Proving what is acceptable unto the Lord.

And have no fellowship with the unfruitful works of darkness, but rather reprove them.

For it is a shame even to speak of those things which are done of them in secret.

But all things that are reproved are made manifest by the light: for whatsoever doth make manifest is light.

Wherefore he saith, Awake thou that sleepest, and arise from the dead, and Christ shall give thee light.

See then that ye walk circumspectly, not as fools, but as wise,

Redeeming the time, because the days are evil.

Wherefore be ye not unwise, but understanding what the will of the Lord is.

And be not drunk with wine, wherein is excess; but be filled with the Spirit;

Speaking to yourselves in psalms and hymns and spiritual songs, singing and making melody in your heart to the Lord;

Giving thanks always for all things unto God and the

Father in the name of our Lord Jesus Christ.

(Ephesians 5:1-26, KJV)

Those of you who work in advertising will be familiar with what I am about to say. It is my understanding that a successful ad addresses one of or a combination of a person's physical appetites: eating, sleeping, having sex, experiencing pleasure, and obtaining power.

With a constant barrage of messages all around us telling us to eat more and better, to sleep more and better, to have more and better sex, to take more pleasure more often, and to have more power over more of our lives, it can be difficult to stay focused and to maintain control. However, being tempted is not the same as acting as if you have no limits, which is always a recipe for disaster.

If we keep our eyes on God, our temptations, while difficult, will be diminished, at least for a while. Will we fail? Of course, we will, but that's where we need space and grace.

While the preceding three things apply to men and women, the next few tips more directly apply to men.

Fourth, biblical manhood includes the responsibility to protect the family, even to the point of the man giving up his life (Ephesians 5:25). Giving up one's life might sound a little extreme, but it does point to the seriousness and the lengths to which a man will go to protect his family. The Book of Nehemiah tells us that men were called upon to fight to protect their wives and children (Nehemiah 4:13-14).

First Peter 3:7 says, "Likewise, ye husbands, dwell with them according to knowledge, giving honor unto the wife, as unto the weaker vessel, and as being heirs together of the grace of life; that your prayers be not hindered." Here I may have to take issue with Peter, because from my experience I can't say that women are weak. True, they may be weaker in physical strength, perhaps, but it takes a strong woman to love a strong man.

The point is, though, that men should treat their wives with respect and honor because men and women are God's heirs, and God plays no favorites. In his eyes, men and women are equally precious and valuable, and Jesus died for everyone.

Fifth, men are called to be the primary providers for their families. However, for many of us, this just can't be the case, and sometimes wives earn more money than their husbands. In an age where many families need at least two people to support their households, it is vital for men to do their share (Genesis 3:17-19).

Sixth, men are leaders within a marriage. It may not mean that they are the sole leader or the leader all the time, because a good leader knows that sometimes it's best to shut up and follow.

A person shouldn't lead because they feel entitled

to but because they are best equipped. As Paul says in Ephesians, a man should lead, taking Jesus Christ as his example through love; through service and sacrifice; and through grace, mercy, and compassion.

God's View of Womanhood

First, women, like men, are also children of God, with all the rights, privileges, and responsibilities that being God's heir entails. **Second**, we all should love our neighbors as ourselves. **Third**, we are all called to control our appetites. However, there are additional things that apply more directly to women.

Fourth, Proverbs 31:10-31 gives us a good description of an ideal wife. Here we see that a godly wife is virtuous and valuable. She is trustworthy and industrious. Not only does she run a tight household, she is also a keen businesswoman. She is smart and makes her husband look good in front of his peers, and she is loved by her husband and children. Interestingly, though, she may not be beautiful, at least on the outside, but she is beautiful on the inside where it counts.

Fifth, women may also be providers and nurturers for the family, but it is also their responsibility to run the household. Anyone who can keep up with children, work, appointments, schedules, bills, sick family members, cooking, cleaning, and the hundreds of other things a household demands knows that it takes more than one person to do it all.

In Bible times, it was assumed that if you were prosperous, you also had servants and/or family nearby or living with you to help with all of those domestic duties. That's usually no longer the case, so keeping the home running smoothly requires everyone in the house to pitch in and help.

Sixth, women are leaders. We sometimes overlook this, and we sometimes forget that there are women in the Bible who were leaders.

Deborah was a judge and a warrior (Judges 4–5). The queen of Sheba was a political leader (1 Kings 10). Miriam, the sister of Moses and Aaron, was a prophet and one of the triad of leaders of Israel during the Exodus from Egypt (Exodus 15:24). Huldah, a prophet and a religious leader, verified the authenticity of the "Book of the Law of the LORD given through Moses"—the Book of Deuteronomy—and she triggered a religious renewal (2 Chronicles 34:22; 2 Kings 22:14).

The Bible shows us that women are fully capable of doing what God calls them to do. Sometimes they have to pick up the slack from men just like sometimes men have to pick up the slack from women.

Dating for a Bigger and Better Marriage

There are ten things we want you to know about dating so that you can find a partner for your bigger and better marriage.

Your makeup. Yes, what you need to know about dating begins with knowing who you are. As a child of God, you are fearfully and wonderfully made (Psalm 139:14). You are precious in God's sight, but don't take this to mean that you should be prideful or boastful about it. A child of God is also humble and self-effacing.

You are a person with worth and value, and you don't chase after anyone who will make you less than who you are in the eyes of God. You are a prize, so don't settle. Get to know yourself and what you have to offer because there is plenty you have to contribute to a dating relationship.

So who are you? If you had to describe yourself in ten words, what would they be? What's your favorite color, movie, car, computer game, sport, or musician? When you know these things about yourself, it is easier to make conversation while you're on a date. I know lots of men who are afraid to be alone with women because they're afraid they won't have anything to talk about. So be prepared.

Maurice was nervous about going out with Carmen. She was so beautiful, and he thought he was lucky she agreed to go to a movie with him. He wasn't nervous about being with her at the movie, but he was scared to death about the time it would take riding in the car there and back.

Maurice was more of an action guy; he wasn't much of a talker. He knew a lot about movies, and the Academy Awards were going to be on TV in a couple of weeks, so maybe they could talk about that.

When Maurice picked up Carmen, the conversation actually went well. She could tell that he was nervous, but she was, too. She also had prepared a few topics to talk about during their time in the car. After they started talking, though, everything went smoothly.

Another helpful thing to know about yourself involves your limits. How many hours of sleep do you need each night? Are you a morning or an evening person? When is your best time of day? Would you rather sit on the sidelines or be down on the field with all the action? Hopefully, this book will help you learn more about yourself as well.

Your mission. Your mission is all about your purpose, passions, and plans. When it comes to dating, you might ask yourself: *Does this person share my passion? How will this person fit into my life and with my friends and family? How important is it that my friends and family like this person? Can I see a future for us?*

Levi and Jeanette met through a mutual friend. When Levi was home for the holidays, he stayed with his parents, but he lived and worked on the West Coast. Levi and

Jeanette tried dating long-distance for a while, but she was unwilling to move to L.A., and he didn't have the kind of job that allowed him to fly back East as often as he would have liked.

The two tried to stay in touch, but it just became too difficult to maintain a relationship over the miles that separated them. So after giving their long-distance relationship a good try, Levi and Jeannette decided they weren't ready to commit and that perhaps it would be better if they started seeing other people. It was painful for both of them, but they believed it was for the best.

Levi was a man on a mission. He intended to make a lot of money and sail the Pacific. It had been his dream and his passion since he was a boy. He decided that maybe it would be best if he didn't date anyone for a while or until he'd accomplished his goal. It wouldn't be fair to any woman he dated if he couldn't make her a priority.

Jeannette was applying to dental school. Being a dentist had been her passion since she fell in love with biology in high school. She decided that her career was going to have to take priority for now. Maybe in a couple of years, she'd call Levi and see where they were with their plans.

Your motive. Why do you want to date? If you want to date with the intention of finding a life partner, you need to ask yourself why.

Amanda believed that she needed a man to complete her life. She didn't need someone simply to share her life. Instead, she thought she needed a man in order for her to be a complete person. In other words, she was needy. As a result, she was always pushing the men she dated for a commitment too early in the relationship.

Amanda knew why she wanted to date, but she was too ready to skip the dating and jump ahead to being married. All she wanted was to get married and have children; and while there was nothing wrong with that, Amanda didn't see herself as an individual first. She saw herself only as someone else's appendage. She had what psychologists call a dependent personality.

Because she always saw herself in someone else's shadow, Amanda didn't think she was worth much. She drove men away in droves, even though she is attractive. Then she found a man who needed to control his partner. At first, Amanda felt happy, safe, and secure; but it wasn't long before the relationship became abusive.

Amanda needed to gain confidence and be out on her own, something her parents had never allowed. Instead, she hooked up with a character guaranteed that she would be stuck under his thumb for as long as they dated.

Luke wanted to date because he was a loving and a giving man. He was looking for the kind of woman who could help take his life to the next level, and he wanted to help take hers to the next level as well. He'd had several long-term relationships that didn't work out, but now he was ready to find "the one." While he knew that no woman was perfect, he believed his life would be better and more fulfilling with a life-long partner.

In the great scheme of things, it helps if people are mature enough to know who they are and what they want out of life before entering into serious dating relationships. Are you dating only for fun, for sex, or to find someone with whom you can build a bigger and better marriage?

Your method. How do you plan to meet the person you want to date? Although I am amazed by how many people meet through websites, it seems to work for some people. There are plenty of other ways to meet people: through friends, family members, work, hobbies, school, and by chance.

While there are hundreds of ways to meet people, what's the best way for you to meet someone you want to date? It depends on your values and your ability to find a person who will share them. So, in my opinion, meeting someone at a bar doesn't usually work out, but church can be a good place to find the kind of person you're looking for. You have to mix with the kind of people you like being around.

Your match. Who attracts you? It's been said that a woman will marry someone like her father, and a man will marry someone like his mother. So if you want to see what your mate will look like in twenty years, look at his or her parents.

While we may not like to admit it, there is some truth to that statement. It's also said that men date blondes and marry brunettes, and women love to date "bad boys" but marry "responsible providers." There is some truth to these statements as well. Unfortunately, some people tend to be attracted to those who will only hurt and disappoint them.

Who we are attracted to says a lot about who we are. Chances are if you are attracted to someone who is bad for you and you know it, you need help.

Zach dated a woman who would not be faithful to him. Try as Zach did to make her love him, she would say she loved him and then leave to be with someone else.

This went on for two years. In all that time, Zach was "true blue" and faithful to his girlfriend until one day it occurred to him that they didn't have a relationship. What had he been thinking? Zach decided to see a counselor for a few sessions to get his head screwed on right and to find out why he'd been so attracted to someone he knew wouldn't treat him right.

Your mantra. What is your dating philosophy? Are you the kind of person who dates someone only two or three times and then moves on? Are you the kind of person who dates multiple people at one time?

Are you the kind of person who dates one person exclusively for extended periods of time but balks at the thought of commitment and marriage? Or are you the kind of person who once you've found someone you see a future with, you go all out to make it happen?

Some of your answers may depend on your age, maturity level, or stage in life. For example, Billie and Jack were in their mid-twenties when they met. Each had had a couple of significant relationships, and Jack had even been engaged once before. However, when they met, it didn't take long before they knew they were right for each other.

They married six months later and have been married for twenty-five years. They knew who they were, who they wanted, and that together they could make a wonderful life.

Let's say, though, you are the kind of person who likes to date around, and you find yourself dating someone who wants to date only you. What should you do? Obviously, you must be honest but also kind. It may be that you're not ready or that you'll never be ready to date someone with the intent to head toward marriage, but you owe it to the other person not to string them along.

Your morals. Morals consist of what you believe to be right and wrong. They are your principles, or your standards, of what you consider good or bad. A moral person is one who is considered to be virtuous, upright, upstanding, high-minded, honorable, honest, just, noble, incorruptible, respectable, and decent. A moral person is one who lives a clean life.

I had a friend who when someone said she looked good considering how old she was would always say, "Honey, it's just clean living."

These days many people come to church so they can learn what a Christian's morals should be. How we are supposed to live is clearly spelled out in the Bible, in fact, that's what the Ten Commandments are—rules to live by. They are listed below.

1. You shall have no other gods before me.

2. You shall not make idols.

3. You shall not take the name of the Lord your God in vain.

4. Remember the Sabbath day, to keep it holy.

5. Honor your father and your mother.

6. You shall not murder.

7. You shall not commit adultery.

8. You shall not steal.

9. You shall not bear false witness against your neighbor.

10. You shall not covet.

When God gave Moses this law, it was not made in a general way because each commandment is directed specifically at individuals. A closer translation of the commandants in Hebrew would read like this:

1. You as an individual shall never, ever have any other gods before me.

2. You as an individual shall never, ever make idols.

3. You as an individual shall never, ever take the name of the Lord your God in vain.

4. You as an individual shall always remember the Sabbath day, to keep it holy.

5. You as an individual shall always honor your father and your mother.

6. You as an individual shall never, ever murder.

7. You as an individual shall never, ever commit adultery.

8. You as an individual shall never, ever steal.

9. You as an individual shall never, ever bear false witness against your neighbor.

10. You as an individual shall never, ever covet.

In Hebrew, these ten sentences are represented as ten words, and each command is addressed to us as individuals. These are ten things we must do without fail if we are to be God's children.

I realize that things happen, and sometimes we are forced to go against our principles for the greater good, but our morals give us a place to stand. Standing, especially when you're standing alone, is uncomfortable. However, as Christians, we know that God plus one is the majority.

So where do you stand? What do you stand for? Knowing this is key to knowing who you are and who you will accept as a potential life partner.

Your mandatories. These are the "must haves," the non-negotiables. One of those "must haves" might be as simple as you won't date anyone who smokes, or perhaps you refuse to date anyone who hates jazz or who loves bowling.

Your "must haves" are up to you, but it's good to be clear what they are. Knowing them can save you a lot of time in finding the right person.

Your map. This is a pragmatic consideration that has to do with your time line. Are you looking for someone now, next year, in ten years? Women especially are sensitive to their biological clocks if they intend to have children. Perhaps you are divorced or have just come out of a serious, long-term relationship and don't want to date someone on the rebound. Perhaps you want to take time to enjoy being single before you enjoy being married.

Your marks. How do you know you've found "the one"? For some people, they know they have found the one when they feel a certain way.

One young man I know said he knew he'd found his true love when it just felt right, like everything just came together. Yes, it was a subjective feeling, but it was necessary for him to feel that way for him to know. You can check things off your list, but if you don't feel a deep connection and an attraction, your relationship is doomed from the start.

---

*Dating is the first step toward having
a bigger and better marriage.*

Deal-Breakers

In your relationship there may come a time when you recognize that you're on the wrong path. Perhaps you've picked the wrong person or that person deceived you in some way. Maybe you've discovered more about yourself and realigned your goals. However, some things are deal-breakers for your relationship.

Here are some of the deal-breakers for Vanessa and me: dishonesty, lack of commitment, unwillingness to invest time, lack of communication, unacceptable habits, ignoring the other person's opinion or beliefs.

Take Away

Dating is only a step, but it is an important step toward having a bigger and better marriage. Dating is a transition from being single to being a couple, and a Christian who enters a dating relationship can begin by seeing himself or herself and potential dates as images of God.

In addition, we must know ourselves—our makeup, mission, motive, method, match, mantra, morals, mandatories, map, and marks.

Offering Space and Grace

1. Share an example of when you needed space. What did you do? How did other people help, or how did they not help?

2. What signals do you give the other person that you need more space or less space? What signals do you like to receive so that you know the other person needs more space or less space?

3. How comfortable are you asking for grace and space? Practice asking your partner for more space. How did it feel to ask for more space? to be asked?

CHAPTER TWO

COMMITMENT FOR A BIGGER AND BETTER MARRIAGE

*Know therefore that the L*ORD *thy God, he is God, the faithful God, which keepeth covenant and mercy with them that love him and keep his commandments to a thousand generations. —Deuteronomy 7:9, KJV*

COMMITMENT FOR A BIGGER AND BETTER MARRIAGE

After you've dated and gotten to know your potential partner, you may begin to think about what's next. Relationships are always moving forward or backward; they are always becoming deeper or shallower. Healthy relationships are always changing and adapting to new circumstances. They are getting bigger and better or smaller and worse.

In a rock-solid relationship, you are loving and growing as individuals and as a couple; but the step into a committed relationship is a transition from the causal "I can do with or without you" to "I've decided that you're the one I want." It's a decision that if not handled with care can cause it all to come tumbling down.

Even so, a commitment to each other and to the relationship has to happen for you to end up with the kind of bigger and better marriage you want. Often a commitment comes as a result of a plateau in your relationship.

Commitment After Your Relationship Plateaus

Maybe this situation has happened to you.

Mary and Sammy have been dating for three years. They are comfortable with each other and enjoy each other's company, but their relationship has just rocked along lazily for over a year. There's nothing wrong, but something isn't exactly right, either.

To Mary, their relationship is beginning to feel stale. From her point of view, Sammy is paying less and less attention to her and taking her for granted. Sammy, on the other hand, wonders where the spark is. Is he still in love with Mary? Sure, he can't see himself with anybody else, but he hasn't been looking, either.

Mary and Sammy's relationship has plateaued. There are times when all relationships get in a rut, and that's where Mary and Sammy are right now. Their relationship isn't growing, which means it's dying because it isn't going anywhere. It just is. If things keep going the way they are, Mary and Sammy won't move on to a rock-solid marriage.

When relationships plateau, it's a signal that it's time for a change. In Mary and Sammy's case, it's time for a deeper commitment. They need to talk about where they are going as a couple, and they may need to confront the things they've avoided dealing with, fearing that if they did, they'd rock the boat.

In Sammy's case, he needs to decide if he cares enough about Mary to make a life with her. Frankly, being with someone forever is scary for him. His parent's marriage only lasted until he was ten, and Sammy is worried about whether he'll make a good father. He's not sure he actually likes children or likes having them around all the time, and he doesn't know how to tell Mary that.

The word forever *scares some people, with good reason.*

Mary has doubts, too. Her fears also concern being a parent. She worries whether she can be the kind of mother she wants to be and still be able to meet the demands of her career. As a child, she hated going to daycare and thinks that a mother should stay at home with her children full-time, at least until they go to school. However, that means she'll lose five years of her career; and in her competitive field, she's not sure she can afford being out so long.

Sammy and Mary are apprehensive about the future, so it's been easier just to go along to get along; but they both feel something has to change. We can glibly say that they should talk and be honest with each other—and they do need to do that. However, that conversation can be difficult to begin because they are afraid of losing what they have.

It took a long time for them to find each other, and neither wants to mess things up. However, if they want their relationship to go deeper and be more solid, they need to confront their fears and anxieties together.

Because this won't be the last plateau that happens to Sammy and Mary, how they address this one now will set the stage for how they deal with plateaus in the future.

In this case, Mary and Sammy are mature adults. They know what they want, and they have a firmly rooted faith. They share enough values that they want the same things out of life; but now they need to make a commitment that will move them forward together, no matter what. Then talking about their differences and their fears won't be as hard.

Believe me, it takes courage to talk things through, and here's why. Sammy isn't going to feel better about his capacity to be a life-long marriage partner and father until he's in that situation. Mary can't know if she'll be able to stay home with the children or even if they'll have any children until it actually happens. The best they can do right now is to discuss possibilities and what ifs, but first they have to decide that they are committed to facing these difficulties together.

It's not that a commitment will "save" them and their relationship, but it will take their relationship to another level. Commitment will give them a better sense of safety that they don't have to be perfect all the time or else one of them will leave. It means that they are more willing to have space and grace for each other.

In a sense, that is one thing dating is all about: finding out if you can give the space and grace the other person needs or if you can grow into being able to do that. Mary and Sammy have dated long enough to know that they want each other as partners, so they are ready to commit to go deeper. Now they have to talk about it to each other face to face.

Pauline and Rick are in a different situation. They were high school sweethearts, and Pauline got pregnant the night of their junior prom. Their parents prevailed in telling the couple they were too young to get married. They reasoned, Why compound one mistake with another?

Rick wanted to go to college, so he went ahead with his plans. Pauline seriously thought about giving up the baby for adoption but couldn't bring herself to do so. Her parents said they would help out, and Rick promised to help, too; but although he loved Pauline, he broke his promise.

Pauline decided to keep the baby and find a way to go to college later. She thought it unfair that she was saddled with all the responsibility for their child. She was angry but resigned.

Rick went to an out-of-state college and found it hard to stay faithful to Pauline, so their relationship was on and off. Despite the help she received from her parents, Pauline couldn't provide for the baby and work and go to school. So she dropped out of school, vowing to go back later.

After Rick graduated, he came home and wanted to pick up with Pauline again "just where they left off." At first, Pauline was happy. It would mean that her child would be raised by two parents, and surely Rick would help out so she could go back to school.

So the couple moved in together. Rick got a job; Pauline went back to school; and the child, no longer a baby, stayed at a neighbor's house during the day. Everything seemed to be working out nicely for a while, but then Rick and Pauline's relationship plateaued. They never talked about her feelings of anger and betrayal or his feelings of anger and guilt, and they both felt trapped. Neither Rick nor Pauline noticed for a while. They were too busy making ends meet.

However, one day, Pauline had had enough and came home from school and announced that she was moving out, leaving the child with Rick. This blindsided him. After all he had done, why was she going to leave him?

Rick and Pauline's relationship plateaued long ago, but neither made the decision to commit to go deeper. They were satisfied with sweeping all their discontent under the rug until one day the stuff under the rug became a mountain of hostility. They just sat in the boat while nobody steered, and their relationship drifted as a result.

They never made a commitment to each other for the space and grace to hear what the other thought. They assumed that having a child together would keep them together. Then their relationship hit the rocks.

Am I saying that they should have gotten married? No, because marriage comes after making a commitment, not before. They never got that far. Yes, they lived together, but that does not constitute a commitment to remain together no matter what, which is foundational to having a rock-solid marriage.

Commitment After Tragedy

Sometimes commitment comes as the result of a tragedy. When Cherie and Julio met, it was a case of love at first sight. They met at church and shared common goals. They had been dating for about six months, and their relationship was great and getting better all the time.

Then Julio's father died unexpectedly. Even though Julio and his father weren't especially close, he took it hard. Cherie had never lost anyone close to her, so this was all new for her; but every time she tried to help, Julio pushed her away. He said he needed to be alone for a while. He told her that it wasn't anything she had done wrong, but he just needed space and grace for a while.

If Cherie had been insecure, she might have taken offense and felt pushed out. However, she realized that while she couldn't rescue him, she could build a wall of protection around him through prayer—and that is what she did.

It didn't happen overnight, but Julio's grief finally subsided enough that he could see what Cherie was doing for him, and he appreciated the space and grace she offered. This made him love her more because he now knew that with Cherie at his side, he could face anything. They made a commitment to each other, and they were married a year later.

What Does Commitment Look Like?

As you might expect, the Bible is big on commitment, and one of the words the Bible uses for "commitment" is *covenant*. In biblical times, making a covenant with someone was serious business. It was a contract and required careful forethought. The parties who made the covenant were making solemn promises to each other. Sometimes they put up collateral, and there were specified penalties if someone backed out of the covenant.

The Hebrew word for "covenant" also means "to cut." So you didn't *make* a covenant, you literally *cut* a covenant— today we might say "cut a deal"—and in biblical times, cutting always involved blood.

We can see how a covenant was made by reading Genesis 15. In this case, the two parties were God and Abraham. While there is some variation, this same procedure was the same as those played out between two people.

A covenant was made when the person of lower status made vows to the person of higher status and said, "If I don't keep my word, so let it be done to me as with this animal." Then the animal was cut in two halves. The person of lower status would walk between the bleeding animal parts to show his firm intent. The person of higher status might also make commitments, but he was not the one who was pledged to die if the terms of the covenant were broken.

In Genesis 15:7-21, God puts Abram (Abram's name was later changed to Abraham, which means "father of the people") to sleep, and God himself, symbolized by a burning lamp, passes between the sacrificed animals. This is an illustration of God's space and grace for us.

God took the burden of keeping the covenant upon himself. He took the role of the person with the lesser status, even though he was God. The promise God pledged to keep was to make Abram a great nation by giving his descendants the Promised Land. This is one place in the Bible that describes God's formal pledge to Abram.

When we make a commitment today, we don't cut animals in half and walk through them. However, making a commitment means that we must be prepared to make sacrifices for the other person in terms of our time, presence, and finances. We are promising in a profound way to do our best to offer our partner the gifts of space and grace.

Will we always get it right? No. Will we make mistakes? Yes. That is part of the human adventure.

When you climb a mountain, you are going up or down. The farther up you go, the better the view because you get a bigger picture. I've seen people rock climb without safety ropes. Maybe you participate in this sport and know what it's like. It amazes me how their fingers always find a crevice to grab onto in order to pull themselves up the rock face.

Rock climbing is too extreme for me, but there are important lessons to learn from the sport. As a climber moves up the mountain, he has to commit. Once committed, there can be no hesitancy. You can't "almost" grab on. You have to commit and go.

Making a commitment to get married is similar. If you believe that this person is right for you and you've tested your thinking by dating for a time, you have to transition your relationship toward a commitment to go to the next level or else your relationship is over. The relationship might drag on and on, but if you're not going deeper and growing as a couple, it won't last and you might as well find someone else.

Money, Sex, and Power

As you think about whether to move forward toward a commitment, there are a few things you need to consider first.

Money

Couples fight over money more than anything else, so you need to think about what money means to both of you. For some, money brings status. It's a symbol of how important they are not only in their own eyes but also in the eyes of others.

Money can put people in certain social circles and in more exclusive groups. It allows them to join certain clubs, attend prestigious events, and rub elbows with important people—the movers and shakers of the world. Others look up to the wealthy and curry for favor. However, having money can also mean other things.

For some people, money provides security and safety. As long as they have money, they believe they are safe from living on the streets or from having to put themselves in compromising positions. Financial security means always having the necessities of life, in whatever way that may be defined.

As you and your partner talk about commitment, you need to know what money means to you. The following scenario will give you an example of how money means different things to two people in a relationship.

Kia and Michael had dated for several months before they had their first fight. On their way to a football game, Michael insisted on parking in the most expensive lot. From Kia's point of view, it wouldn't hurt them to walk a little, but Michael insisted.

Michael thought that since he was paying for everything, it should be his decision, and Kia couldn't argue with that. He had also bought great seats on the 50-yard line, and he beamed as he made his way past his friends who were on their way to the nosebleed section.

By the time they got back to Kia's place, she was livid. Where did Michael come off trying to look like such a big shot? In her way of thinking, he could have spent some of the money he wasted on the game to fix up his apartment. However, Michael saw nothing wrong with what he did. To him, money means status, and if he has money, he is going to make sure other people know it.

From his perspective, Michael thought Kia was stingy. He knew that she grew up not having much and that she thought of money as security, which would protect her from ever wanting again. But Michael couldn't understand why she couldn't just let go and have some fun and enjoy spending money sometimes.

As Michael and Kia argued over his wastefulness and her stinginess, it finally occurred to them that money meant different things to them. If their relationship was going to keep going toward the possibility of a rock-solid marriage, they would have to compromise.

Michael would have to give Kia grace when she criticized him, and she would have to give him space to splurge once in a while. He would have to realize that all she was asking for was for him to be more responsible with money, and she would have to realize that all he was asking for was for the freedom to have fun.

As they move toward a commitment to marry, couples need to discuss what money means and how they plan to deal with it together. For example:

- Will they have a joint bank account, or should they keep their money separate?

- What are the debts each person is bringing into the marriage, and how are those debts being paid?

- Who will pay the bills, and how will that person divide the financial responsibilities? Who is primarily responsible for making investment decisions?

- Will the couple make a budget? Who will make it, and who will be responsible for keeping it?

- What did money mean in the couples' families of origin?

- Do they want to put their money toward certain things, such as a vacation or a new car?

- Will they designate money for each of them to "play" with?

- Who is primarily responsible for figuring and paying the taxes?

Making decisions on these matters doesn't mean that things won't change down the road, but discussing these issues now helps couples set the groundwork for handling money wisely and avoiding confrontations and disagreements.

Sex

Although it seems that most people have sex before marriage these days, having sex before being in a committed relationship is a recipe for disaster. For years, psychologists have said that when two people engage in sexual intimacy, they form a bond. This bond is emotional and physical.

There is no such thing as casual sex or sex that doesn't mean anything because God didn't make us that way. Sex always means something, even though it might mean different things to different people.

Whether you are a man or a woman, when you are intimate with someone, there is a lasting physiological bond that takes place. While it's true that physical intimacy means different things to men and women, and sexual intimacy is more than physical closeness, it's also true that in the sexual act, two people become one.

Then when two people break up, their oneness is torn apart. They are then left with emotional wounds that will eventually scar, making the next sexual encounter with another person more difficult.

Over time, when a person has bonded, been torn apart, been wounded, and been scarred so often, true intimacy with anyone becomes impossible. That is a tragedy of prostitution and promiscuity. So if sex means nothing to you, maybe you've had so many sexual encounters that you can't have true intimacy with anyone. If that is your situation, you need to seek help.

Sex is a gift from God. He is not anti-sex, but he doesn't want people to have sex without commitment and, if possible, marriage.

God means for sex to enhance and enrich your life, so you and your partner need to have a frank conversation about sex. Vanessa and I are not naïve. We know that hormones can make people do crazy things. However, for sex to be satisfying for both partners, each person needs to feel valued and respected by the other. Sex is always more than a physical act, especially for women, but not just for women.

In the sexual act, you make yourself vulnerable to your partner, and both of you need to feel valued and appreciated for who you are as whole persons. Sex is not just about particular body parts. Those parts, after all, are connected to a complete body and a spirit.

For some people, being seen without their clothes is difficult because they have poor body image and don't feel comfortable in their own skin. For example, in an episode of *Downton Abbey*, Mr. Carson, the butler, and Mrs. Hughes, the housekeeper, decide to marry. They are an older couple, and the issue that almost breaks the deal is that Mrs. Hughes is afraid for Mr. Carson to see her naked. She claims she's not beautiful, and she fears he will be disappointed or completely turned off.

It's not only older couples who worry about these sexual situations. Women as well as men have body image issues, so it is necessary to give your partner space and grace and help your partner feel accepted enough that over time both of you will grow to feel more comfortable in your vulnerability.

Power

You might ask, "What's power got to do with it?" but in any relationship there is a balancing of power that is always taking place. People use such things as money and sex to manipulate and maneuver their partners to do what they want them to do.

Many years ago, I counseled with two people who were experiencing a problem with the balance of power in their relationship. She was a little younger than her partner, but she was bright and, to all appearances, a confident, mature woman. Her partner was an important man in his social circle and had a prestigious job, and she stood in awe of him.

He loved her, but she felt so small when she compared herself to him. His "big personality," as she put it, made her feel protected, but it was also a little scary. She had always been the dominant person in her dating relationships. This was new to her, and it felt right, even though she thought it would take time for her to get used to it.

She knew that between the two of them he held most of the power. Surprisingly, when she told him that, he was floored. He felt in awe of her, too. He thought she had the "big personality." This discovery signaled to them that power was important in their relationship because they were both so sensitive to it. So they needed to keep checking in with each other to see how the other felt.

In most relationships there is shared power, but it's not always 50/50. Actually, this is a good thing because people are good at different things and at handling particular situations. However, it is important to monitor who holds the power because some people enjoy power a little too much.

Jay was the manager of a construction company. His employees liked him because he was a decisive, no-nonsense sort of boss. He barked out orders, and the shop ran smoothly as a result. However, when he came home, Jay was the same guy. He barked out orders, but he didn't get the same response.

Jay was married to Eve, who had three children from a previous marriage. Jay had two children from a previous marriage, and he and Eve had a baby together. Theirs was a blended family. Eve stayed home cooking, cleaning, and doing everything else a parent does, including looking after all six kids, who lived with them.

However, Jay couldn't understand why his home wasn't like his business. He was liked and respected at work, but at home it was a different story.

Jay was used to being in control, and he liked being the boss. He was comfortable with having all the power—in fact, that's what he preferred. However, it wasn't until they came to counseling that Eve was able to tell Jay in a way that he would hear that she didn't want to be treated like one of his employees, as an underling. She was his wife and wanted to be treated as an equal partner. In a power move of her own, Eve manipulated Jay into going to counseling by withholding sex.

After thinking about what Eve was saying in their counseling sessions, Jay remembered his first wife saying the same things to him years before. While it was difficult for him to learn to share power, he made the effort, and his and Eve's home life improved substantially.

Eve also had to learn that withholding sex was a manipulative power move. She was not as powerless as she thought she was, but there were better ways to address problems in their relationship.

Deal-Breakers

You are never going to know everything about a person before you get married. In fact, you won't begin to know what marriage is like until you first decide to commit to your relationship. However, there are also signs that you should not move forward with a commitment.

These are some of the deal-breakers couples face:

1. You don't communicate well with each other.
2. You can't get past the other person's history.
3. You can't get past parental philosophies.
4. Your financial practices are too different.

5. There are signs and signals of domestic violence.
6. You have totally opposite goals and objectives.
7. The other person tries to isolate you from friends and family.
8. The other person has a negative influence on you.
9. You get or give the other person sporadic attention and attendance.
10. Your religious conflicts cannot be resolved to your satisfaction.

Take Away

Commitment is the important transition between dating and having a bigger and better marriage. Things won't be the same after marriage as they were before you got married. But without commitment, neither of you can give the other the space and grace needed to make your relationship work like it needs to in order for you to face all the storms life will hurl at you.

Space and grace build a protective hedge or wall around your relationship. This protective wall is not meant to keep you captive but to give you the opportunity and the safety to be who you are.

Offering Space and Grace

1. In your opinion, what's the best way for couples to avoid fighting over money? What works or doesn't work for you as a couple?

2. Sex is a gift from God. How might knowing this change your view of sex?

3. Do you believe premarital sex is OK? How long should a couple be together before they have sex? How will they know the time is right?

4. Is sex and intimacy different for men and women? Why or why not?

5. In your opinion, how does commitment change a relationship? What are ways couples show each other that they are committed to the relationship?

6. If you are going on a date, who makes the decisions about where to go? Who usually pays?

7. If a couple decides not to see each other anymore, what's the best way to break up?

CHAPTER THREE

PRELUDE TO A BIGGER AND BETTER MARRIAGE

Therefore shall a man leave his father and his mother, and shall cleave unto his wife: and they shall be one flesh.

—Genesis 2:24, KJV

PRELUDE TO A BIGGER AND BETTER MARRIAGE

Renee had dreamed of her wedding her entire life. Ever since she was a little girl she'd made plans for this day. Her Barbie and Ken dolls still wore their bridal attire, even though they had been packed away for years; and she had created Pinterest boards full of ideas for a dress, rings, decorations, various music groups to play at the reception, and dozens of photos from luxurious honeymoon destinations. Renee knew exactly what she wanted, and she was intent on having it her way.

Roberto loved Renee and was willing to do what he could to make her dreams come true; but he and Renee were paying for the wedding, and he didn't want to go into a lot of debt for one day—even a day as important as their wedding day. Still, he was willing to give her space and grace so she could have her dream wedding.

Renee and Roberto started dating during college and continued to date for a couple of years after graduation. When they decided they wanted to take their relationship to the next level, they had a long talk and decided that marriage was their next step.

Renee didn't want to move in with Roberto. Although Renee had a hard time explaining her decision to her friends, Roberto knew she was just like that, and he respected her for it. They set a wedding date, and Renee began planning.

The transition from just talking about getting married to actually planning to get married changed their relationship. Soon Renee and Roberto looked at each other differently. Renee thought about what kind of father Roberto would be, and Roberto thought about all the great sex he and Renee would have. He thought they would have their own place and wouldn't have to worry whether his roommate would barge in.

To be fair, Roberto did think about the kind of mother Renee would be, but only a little. In his mind, having children was way down the road.

Premarriage counseling is helpful to iron out differences you might not talk about otherwise.

Because Renee and Roberto wanted to get married in the church and have their pastor perform the ceremony, the pastor was one of the first people they told about their engagement. The pastor had known them since they were in college and had started attending his church.

Pastor Lewis thought Renee and Roberto made a fine pair. He suggested that to do things right, they needed at least four sessions of premarriage counseling. In the state in which they lived, premarriage counseling would give them a discount on the cost of the marriage license. If only to humor Pastor Lewis, Renee and Roberto agreed to go through counseling.

Premarriage Counseling
First Session

Renee and Roberto showed up at the pastor's office right on time, ready to go. That was always a good sign to Pastor Lewis. He invited the couple in, showed them where to sit, and offered them coffee. The couch in the pastor's study was more like a loveseat, and Renee and Roberto sat close to each other. *Another good sign*, Pastor Lewis noted.

After years of providing counseling, Pastor Lewis had observed that a couple's body language spoke volumes. He once had a couple come in and sit at opposite ends of the couch, putting as much distance between themselves as possible. He had another couple who, once they sat down, each pulled out their cell phones and started texting other people.

From his experience, Pastor Lewis had learned that the signals couples give off when they don't want to be close indicate trouble. When a couple's first thought is to keep their friends informed about something so private as a counseling session, that serves as a harbinger for trouble down the road.

However, Renee and Roberto seemed to be on a solid path. To make sure they weren't interrupted, Pastor Lewis asked them to turn off their phones. Roberto looked amused, and Renee flushed a little with guilt, but they turned off their phones and put them away.

Roberto spoke first. "Pastor, we're happy to meet with you, but we already know what we want. Do we really need four sessions of counseling?" Renee nodded in agreement.

Pastor Lewis thought for a moment and said, "I realize you're ready to get married, and you've decided to take your relationship to the next level. For most couples, there can be a lot of fun in dreaming and planning together. Trust me, we'll get to all that. But part of my job is to make sure you touch all the bases. It's easy to do the fun stuff, but there are also hard things you also need to consider."

Roberto and Renee looked worried, but Pastor Lewis continued. "I'm not here to tell you one way or the other, because you've already decided to get married. But I want your marriage to be solid and long-lasting, and I may be able to help you think through some things and talk about them together in a safe place with no interruptions."

Renee and Roberto felt better but wondered what Pastor Lewis had in mind. Most of their friends had just gotten married at the courthouse and celebrated afterward with a big party at a nearby hotel.

Pastor Lewis said, "Don't worry. I think you'll find premarriage counseling helpful. We will spend time discussing details about the ceremony, but first tell me a little about yourselves." He gave them each a sheet of paper and a pen. "Write down ten words to describe yourself." After they finished, Renee and Roberto were a little surprised when they shared their lists.

Then Pastor Lewis told them to turn their papers over and said, "Write ten words to describe your partner. Don't worry, you won't have to share all of them in front of me, but I do hope you will share them with each other later."

Renee looked over the words she used to describe Roberto. It was quite a list, and she was proud of the kind of person Roberto was; but when she shared a couple of her words, Roberto looked at her in disbelief.

"That's what you really think? Do you really think that I'm successful?"

"Yes," Renee said cautiously.

"Wow!" was Roberto's only response.

Then Roberto shared a few of the words he'd written down about Renee. One of them was *willful*. Renee wasn't altogether pleased with this. Roberto tried to explain, but Pastor Lewis cut them off.

"It's important to understand how each of you sees the other, but don't get all hung up on the exact words. The point is that you have a lot more to learn about each other. That's good, actually, because marriage is just the beginning. Nobody knows everything going in. That's the adventure of it."

But Roberto knew that he still had some explaining to do later.

Pastor Lewis smiled at the couple. "Look, knowing who you are as individuals and who you want to be as a couple is important. It's important to talk about, even though some of it will make you uncomfortable." Then he explained how even in bigger and better marriages, relationships plateau, which indicates that choices will need to be made whether to go deeper and climb higher, not slide down the mountain and fall apart.

Roberto and Renee nodded and recognized that the kind of plateau the pastor was talking about had prompted them to decide to get married. A decision to keep climbing was the reason they were in the pastor's study now.

Second Session

Renee and Roberto arrived separately for the second session. Roberto arrived first, which is the way he had planned it. He wanted a couple of minutes alone with the pastor before Renee arrived.

"Pastor," Roberto began, "can I ask you something before Renee gets here?"

Pastor Lewis smiled and nodded.

Roberto cleared his throat and said, "We had a big fight after we left your office last week. You might remember that I said Renee was willful. Well, she didn't like that, which led to, well, a fight. I'm still not sure she has forgiven me, and I don't even know what I did wrong."

"Are you saying that this is the first time this has happened to you?" Pastor Lewis asked.

"Yes. Usually, I just give Renee what she wants, and we go on our merry way. I don't like confrontation. I grew up with fighting in my house, and I vowed that my home would be a place of peace."

"Which means that you just give in while your anger smolders."

"You've got the picture."

"OK," Pastor Lewis said. "I was going to wait until later to bring this up, but tonight we'll talk about family history."

Couples bring their memories and family experiences into the marriage, for better or for worse.

Renee breezed in the door. "Sorry. Traffic was awful," she said.

"Not a problem," Pastor Lewis said. "Tonight, let's talk about your families of origin. I'd like you to diagram your family history, and I'll help you. Renee, you're in social work, so you'll recognize this."

"Yes," Renee said, "It's a genogram."

For the next thirty minutes, Renee and Roberto filled in their genograms. It was an interesting exercise because Roberto learned new things about himself and about Renee. He learned some of the things they had in common. Both of their paternal grandfathers died at an early age, and both of them had disabled cousins.

However, it was a real eye-opener to Roberto when Renee described the heart disease that ran in her family, making her afraid that she might die at an early age, too. That was one of the reasons she adamantly insisted that things always had to be done now because she was afraid she might not get a second chance.

In listening to Roberto, Renee learned that his parents had been married twice—both times to each other—and that there was a lot of anger and fighting during that time. A light-bulb clicked on in her head: So that was one of the reasons he hated when other people got angry.

"You know, Pastor, that was really helpful. I had no idea!" Renee looked at Roberto and said, "So when you told me I am willful, it was hard for you because you thought I'd get angry—and I did. I'm sorry."

Pastor Lewis said, "Knowing who you are and what you bring to a marriage will help you give space and grace to yourself and to each other. There's a lot more work we could do with the genograms, but I invite you to take them home and talk about your families. See what pops up. Compare notes. See how you're alike and how you're different."

Pastor Lewis went on to explain that, like it or not, we all bring our families of origin with us into our marriages. Our home life growing up acts as the scenery backdrop on a stage.

The scenery provides the context and lets the actors and audience take certain things for granted, for example, if the play is taking place in war-torn Iraq or in a ski lodge in Vail, Colorado. In much the same way, our homes set the scene or context for what we expect to happen without having to think anything about it.

Renee grew up in an older house that had only one bathroom. There were five people in the house, so the morning bathroom schedule was meticulously worked out. Everybody had twenty minutes to spend in the bathroom, but Renee always got up first so she could take longer if she needed to. For her, having two or more bathrooms would have been a luxury.

On the other hand, Roberto grew up in a house with two and a half baths. After he learned the conditions in which Renee grew up, it occurred to him that his home life had caused Renee to assume that he and his family were well-off financially.

Renee's grandfather came to live with her family when she was in elementary school, so he was always around when she was growing up. However, when he came to live with them, it meant that Renee and her sister could never parade around the house in their underwear. With the exception of his mother, Roberto lived in a house with all males, so it was nothing for him to run out of the bathroom without a towel wrapped around himself.

Pastor Lewis explained that studying a genogram is good not only for couples about to get married but for those who are already married. When new situations arise, the genogram can show couples new things and help them remember stories they've forgotten.

In fact, just a few days before his counseling session with Roberto and Renee, Pastor Lewis and his wife started discussing and then arguing over what they should do about a beloved elderly aunt. It wasn't until they thought about their respective families that they discovered why their conversation had become so heated. They each had had different experiences with retirement centers. He had horror stories, but his wife had good stories.

Pastor Lewis's experience confirms an important point for couples to remember. The family stories, traditions, and even jokes you bring with you into a marriage are great resources for your relationship in the here and now.

As Renee and Roberto studied their genograms, they had several "aha!" moments. There were lightbulbs coming on all over the place. As they learned more about each other and about themselves as a couple, they grew closer and were able to laugh and cry together.

Although sometimes unbelievable, the things Roberto and Renee shared just had to be true because nobody could make up stories like that. Roberto shared the time when he and his brother got into a fight. Their parents weren't home, and during the fight their mother's favorite vase fell off the mantel and broke into a million pieces.

For the next four hours, the brothers worked feverishly trying to glue the vase back together. They put the vase back in place just as their mother opened the front door.

Much to the brothers' surprise, their mother never said a word about the hastily glued vase. Being children who believed themselves to be smarter than what they were, they thought they were off the hook. Of course, they weren't, but their mother let them think they were. After a few days, though, Roberto's mother politely presented him and his brother with a bill for $100.

As Roberto recounted this story, Renee laughed. She could picture all of it happening just as he said it did. Roberto laughed, too. Looking back on the incident, it was funny now, but it wasn't so funny back then.

Still laughing, Renee shared the story of how she once got even with her older brother. One day after school, they were out in the cow pasture. Dicky, her brother, was taunting Renee as usual, but unbeknownst to him, their prize-winning bull was slowly coming up behind him. Suddenly, Renee threw a rock at the bull and took off running. Since she already had her hiding spot picked out, she was safe in no time. Her brother, however, wasn't so lucky.

Fortunately for Dicky, a neighbor saw what happened and got him to safety before anything serious occurred, but he was so frightened that he wet his pants. However,

Renee felt vindicated for all the teasing she had endured.

Roberto sat in awed silence, and then he broke out laughing. He was amused that little Renee had gotten the better of her bullying older brother by enticing the bull to run after him. Roberto admired that. They both had a good laugh. Maybe this premarriage counseling thing was a good idea after all.

Third Session

At the beginning of the third session, Pastor Lewis announced that the session's topics were money, sex, and power. He introduced the discussion by saying, "You probably know that couples fight about money more than anything else. You probably also know that sex and power are next in line. We'll get to all of that, but first we need to help prevent any future disagreements about those things in the first place. So we're going to talk about your mission as a couple."

Pastor Lewis explained that just as important as it is to have goals and to make plans as individuals, it is also helpful to do those same things as a couple. Vanessa and I have worked and reworked our mission over the years. Our mission is to maximize communication while minimizing concealment. By doing this, we cultivate real respect for each other's feelings and opinions, while simultaneously erasing an environment of merely existing, which ultimately equals merger and not marriage.

We want our original pursuit to love each other more

never to be lost or to diminish over the years. Simply put, we want to keep the same excitement we had while we were dating.

Creating a mission for your marriage
will unite you in a common purpose.

People understand a mission in different ways, but as we see it, a mission is basically the big picture of what you want your marriage to look like, and it can include tactics you might want to use to achieve your dreams. Some marriage experts suggest that it might be important to write your mission out.

However you approach casting the vision and mission of your marriage, remember that both of you need to agree. If you want your mission to be successful, it can't be coerced from the other person or begrudgingly agreed upon. Your mission as a couple needs to contain enough space and grace so it can adapt as your situation changes.

I know of a company where the CEO was insistent on forecasting using three-year plans. The executives endured this ordeal every year. To some of them, it seemed as if that was all they did—prepare for the series of meetings to set their three-year plan, sit through a series of meetings to draft their three-year plan, and sit through another round of meetings to finalize their three-year plan.

To make the annual ordeal easier to endure, one of the

executives figured out the formula of change between the three-year plans. It saved her time but made the planning completely worthless—which it was anyway.

Making a mission statement for your marriage isn't meant to be a pointless ordeal with steps you slavishly follow. Instead, a mission is meant to set the context for how you deal with issues related to money, sex, and power in your relationship.

In the last chapter, we discussed issues related to *money*. Knowing your mission can help you make those decisions. For example, if you are going into a marriage with college debt, what is the priority for paying off that debt in relation to purchasing the things you need? Or if you're planning to buy a house or relocate, are you going to open a special account for savings dedicated specifically to your move?

In the grand scheme of things, how important is it to have a house? What are your goals for fulfilling that dream? Do you pay off the college debt first, or do you put some of your money in savings and some of it toward paying debts? What about a vacation? Where does paying for a vacation fall in line with your financial priorities? If you agree and have a mission, it will be easier (but not necessarily easy) to make these kinds of decisions.

You might be wondering what I could possibly say about *sex*. You might have heard that your sexual relationship will change over time. This is true, but like anything else you will do successfully there must be intentionality, which can be summed up as communication, consideration, and cooperation.

Sexually, you must get to know what your mate likes and dislikes. Then you must work at making what's bad smaller while making what's good bigger and better. It is God's will that we all abstain from sex before marriage; however, there are those who became Christians after losing their virginity. Still others who are Christians, nevertheless, have had premarital sex.

Thank God for his grace and mercy, but I also believe that no level of premarital sex can compare to sex that complies with God's will, which is within marriage. When married couples practice communication, consideration, and cooperation, then they are able to experience God's best in the bedroom. As a bonus, they can say what unmarried couples can't say at the end of a sexual encounter without fear of being struck by lightning: "Thank you, Jesus!"

In marriage, *power* means that sometimes one partner will be the leader, and sometimes the other will be the leader. A mission statement can be helpful here, too, to help you set priorities.

One of the most challenging things couples have to deal with these days is the kind of house they would like to purchase. Rachel and Bob were just starting out, but from the beginning they knew that for Bob to advance up the company ladder, they would have to relocate from time to time. Rachel's career could also require them to move.

So in their mission statement, Bob and Rachel stated that they wanted a warm, welcoming home with one of them at home with their children. They knew that making or turning down a move might damage their career prospects, but family would come first.

Pete and Claire decided differently. They decided that Pete had the best prospects for advancement, so his job and decisions about his job would have to come first. Claire was flexible, having grown up as an Army brat, and she was a teacher, which is something needed anywhere.

The couple's mission was to support the person with the best chance to earn a big salary. A comfortable nest egg was their primary goal, so it made sense to them that Pete's job took priority.

Power in a relationship can also be defined by who is the most dominant. Sadly, some people interpret this to mean physical dominance. It's the old idea that "might makes right." For too many couples this can mean that the bigger person beats up, bullies, or bosses the other, smaller person.

As adults, we know this behavior is childish. We are God's precious children, so there's no excuse to beat up each other physically or emotionally; but sometimes life pushes us hard, and we find our backs against the wall.

We feel that we can't get through to the other person in any other way than to slap or hit them.

If you ever feel like that, it takes the bigger person to walk away, take a time-out, and put a lot of space between you and the other person until you cool down. But let me be clear: *Hitting your spouse is never OK. Never! Never!*

Here is where what you bring into a marriage can affect your own behavior in your marriage. About 40 years ago, Manny, a friend of mine, went to the local hardware store, a place where the neighborhood men hung out. When Manny, entered the store, he heard the men laughing uproariously.

"You should have seen her face!" one of the men hollered.

"You know, sometimes you just have to slap your wife around a little for her to catch on," another man said and then gave the man standing next to him a high-five. All the men laughed even more.

Keep in mind that this incident happened 40 years ago. You might say that that was then, and this is now; but if you've grown up thinking it's acceptable to hit your spouse, abusive actions are in your behavior repertoire somewhere. You might have grown up thinking that that's just the way it is, and under pressure you might slip back to acting that way.

However, I'm here to tell you that it's not OK, and that's not how it is or how it has to be. Christian men and women don't hit each other. Period. End of discussion.

At this point, it might be helpful to say what we mean when we talk about mature people. Here is what a mature person looks like:

- Mature people do not need to hurt an opponent unnecessarily, and aggression subsides when the goal in question is reached. This is opposed to immature people who exhibit hatred and cruelty in the elimination of human obstacles to achieve a goal.
- Mature people enter into interpersonal relationships for mutual joy and fulfillment, not merely for a personal satisfaction of pleasure.
- Mature people become increasingly objective in relation to themselves, their problems, and the problems of others.
- Mature people experience joyful pride and creative achievement in significant relationships that continue to deepen and broaden in scope.
- Mature people can give and receive empathic responses to and from others without threatening their own self-boundaries.
- Mature people are usually altruistic. They are committed to selfless, humanistic behavior, not rooted in the pangs of guilt or in an unacknowledged selfish desire for admiration or immortal reputation. They completely commit themselves to advancing the greater good. They are not "neurotic" because they have no driving desire to avoid guilt or shame for doing otherwise. They are not out for personal

glory or to be revered by society, and they simply and nobly choose to subordinate their own selfish desires for the good of all. While none of us are perfect, nevertheless, we walk this path.

Fourth Session

In their fourth and final session, Renee and Roberto went over the wedding ceremony details with Pastor Lewis. They also went over the church guidelines so they could all be on the same page about what was and wasn't OK.

Pastor Lewis explained that he never expected any problems but that he found having guidelines a helpful practice. All the church wanted was to welcome them and their guests and to make sure everything ran smoothly.

Renee was fine with all the guidelines but pressed Pastor Lewis about the need for them. He told them a true story to illustrate.

When he was a young pastor in his first church, he mistakenly assumed that most weddings were pretty much the same until the mayor's daughter decided to have her wedding at his church. It was a free-for-all. The wedding planner took all the Bibles and hymnals out of the pews because, she said, their color clashed with the bride's wedding colors.

Then the wedding planner started moving the pulpit furniture and other things around in the sanctuary so there'd be enough room for the twelve bridesmaids and twelve groomsmen. (Did I mention that the church was small and could only hold about 250 people?) There wasn't a lot of room to work with, but Pastor Lewis stopped the wedding planner in her tracks when she and a couple of her helpers climbed a ladder so they could remove the sanctuary's cross. He simply wasn't going to let that happen.

To make a long story short, the wedding planner, the bride's mother, and the bride were such a nuisance that after the wedding the deacons insisted that the church establish guidelines for hosting weddings.

As Renee and Roberto were about to wind things up with Pastor Lewis, the pastor said that there was one other piece of advice he needed to give them, and it concerned the honeymoon.

After the Honeymoon

For most couples, the honeymoon is something they will always treasure. After getting through the hectic pace of the ceremony and the reception, dealing with family, and seeing old friends, the honeymoon should be a time when the couple can relax and just enjoy being together. However—and this is what Pastor Lewis wanted to tell Renee and Roberto—nothing can live up to all of the couple's expectations.

"Renee, you want the perfect wedding. Roberto, you know you have the perfect bride. But something is going to happen that will upset that perfection. I'm not talking about something like the videographer not showing up on time, even though I guarantee that there'll be a hitch in the ceremony somewhere. No, I'm talking about your expectations of each other. Maybe the sex won't be right, maybe Roberto will snore so loudly that you won't be able to sleep, or maybe Renee will throw up from bad shrimp. I don't know, but something will happen."

"OK," said Roberto, "we get it. So why the big warning?"

"Because if you don't work through and deal with it, it will become a stumbling block in your relationship."

"That sounds a little scary," Renee said.

"I don't mean to scare you, but I've seen too many couples who don't deal with their disappointment and end up in divorce a few years later. All I'm saying is just be aware, and if you need to talk about whatever happens, give me a call, and we can schedule a time to meet," Pastor Lewis said.

Renee and Roberto didn't understand Pastor Lewis's concern at that time, but after the honeymoon, they did.

Take Away

Deciding to get married is a big step, and it marks a transition in your relationship. While it's best to seek premarriage counseling, if you don't or can't, talk through the issues in this chapter. If you're already married, it never hurts to revisit your mission, attitudes, and behavior regarding money, sex, and power.

Remember that nothing ever goes completely according to plan—not with the ceremony and not with your expectations of the other person—But marriage puts you on the road to a Bigger and Better marriage.

Offering Space and Grace

1. How do couples know that it's time to get married?

2. How might premarriage counseling be helpful for some couples? Why might some people not want premarriage counseling? Who would you feel most comfortable with providing you with premarriage counseling? How might that change if a person has been married more than once?

3. Describe yourselves as a couple. What words best describe your relationship?

4. How does your partner make you a better person?

5. Describe where you think you'll be in five years, twenty years, and in fifty years.

6. How does your family history help or hurt the prospects for your marriage?

7. What do you most look forward to about getting married?

CHAPTER FOUR

CHILDREN AND A BIGGER AND BETTER MARRIAGE

Take heed that ye despise not one of these little ones; for I say unto you,

That in heaven their angels do always behold the face of my Father which is in heaven.

—Matthew 18:10, KJV

CHILDREN AND A BIGGER AND BETTER MARRIAGE

Children evoke such different responses from people. Many people consider young children a nuisance (especially on an airplane), while others love all the babies they see and never fail to rush to pick them up.

Once, when a young bride was about to walk down the aisle with her father, she asked him what he was thinking about. She wanted to hear something warm and fuzzy as befitted the occasion. She wanted to hear him say how proud he was of her, but he simply said, "Children will bring you more joy than you can imagine or break your heart." Then he winked at her and said. "Today it's all joy. Let's go," and down the aisle they went.

The well-known nursery rhyme says:

> Girl and boy sitting in a tree.
> K-I-S-S-I-N-G
> First comes love,
> then comes marriage,
> then comes baby in the baby carriage.

For many couples, children are part and parcel of what a bigger and better marriage is about and the home it provides. However, children will bring new adventures, and if you and your spouse don't have a solid marriage, things between you can get rocky.

When children enter the picture, the relationship between a couple changes. Children represent a transition that can spur you to climb even higher together, or it can dash your hopes on the rocks below. The reason is straightforward, at least with the first baby: Two become three—a couple becomes a threesome, a family. However, for many people this transition is difficult to negotiate.

Children change everything.

Yolanda and Bert had been happily married for three years. They had their mission and stuck with their goals. Everything seemed perfect—and then the baby came. The women at the baby shower told Yolanda that her life would never be the same, and the guys on Bert's pick-up ball team told him that he'd better get ready for change. However, neither of them thought their lives would be that much different.

They both came from big families and even worked with the youth at church. They also had many friends who had children. Everybody said Bert and Yolanda would be great parents. They loved each other, and they already loved their baby. They thought if their friends could do it, so could they. But as all parents know, you can't know until it happens to you.

Yolanda had a long, difficult labor, and the doctor stitched her up tightly afterward. She had decided to nurse the baby and take off three months from work, but the baby didn't readily take to breastfeeding and seemed to prefer bottled formula.

At every turn, it seemed to Yolanda, things weren't going according to plan. Then there was getting up in the middle of the night multiple times to feed the baby. She didn't do well without sleep, but it had to be her because she wanted the baby to nurse.

Bert saw Yolanda put on a brave face every day, and he knew she was worn out, but someone had to keep going to work. Although he wasn't sleeping well, either, he knew he would have to be the one to continue working. One day, his co-workers found him curled up under his desk, asleep.

A few weeks went by, and Bert and Yolanda's schedule became more normal, but this normal was new. The new normal wasn't anything like the old normal; it wasn't like it was before. In the past when Bert came home, Yolanda would already be home preparing dinner. They would eat, clean up the kitchen, and cuddle on the couch as they watched TV.

However, after the baby's arrival, that routine was gone. Now when Bert got home, he had to cook, clean up, and sometimes start the laundry because Yolanda had decided to use cloth diapers for the baby. When Bert hit the bed, he was out. It didn't matter, though, because the couple hadn't had sex for months.

Soon it was time for Yolanda's and the baby's six-week check-ups. Both passed with flying colors. Yolanda's OB/ GYN asked if Yolanda and Bert had had sex since the birth of the baby. Yolanda said that they had tried, but it was too painful, and she asked the doctor if this was normal. The doctor said it was not altogether uncommon, but it would take some time so she should be patient.

When Yolanda got home, Bert excitedly asked her what the doctor had said about having sex. Hearing his question, Yolanda broke down and cried. In frustration, Bert turned and walked away, slamming the door behind him. *Who knew parenthood would be like this?* they thought.

Slowly, things improved for Bert and Yolanda. The baby decided he liked to nurse. In fact, he liked it so much that he wanted to nurse all the time. Yolanda asked her mother, her mother-in-law, and the pediatrician about the baby's nursing habits, and they all confirmed that some babies are like that.

Then there was the couple's concern about their physical and sexual intimacy. Because Yolanda held the baby in her arms much of the time and was busy tending to his needs, there wasn't a lot of time to be physically close to Bert. Now Bert was beginning to feel left out.

It used to be only the two of them—Bert and Yolanda—but now it was Yolanda and the baby and maybe him sometimes. Bert tried not to but he was starting to resent the baby because he felt as if he was being replaced and that Yolanda didn't have time for him anymore.

When Bert confided in a friend what was going on at home, his friend just laughed. What did Bert think having a baby would be like? His friend's exact words were, "Say goodbye to sex for a while." Despite his feelings, Bert loved the baby, and he saw Yolanda blossom into a wonderful mother. He just wanted to be more included in his new family.

Yolanda was busy just trying to keep her head above water. Who knew that a baby dirtied that many clothes or had to be changed so often? She felt overwhelmed, and she was angry with Bert for pouting and feeling left out. She thought he should just grow up and get over it. She could only take care of one baby.

Having a baby was a difficult transition for Yolanda and Bert, and both of them needed to give the other more space and grace. But because they stuck to their mission and kept talking with each other, their marriage grew stronger despite their trials. Like Bert's Army buddy said, "What doesn't kill you makes you stronger."

Blended-Family Issues

Miriam was a lovely divorcée with no children. She and Benny met at the bank where she worked. They dated casually because Miriam wasn't too keen on becoming committed to a man who already had two children, and she wanted to make sure Benny wasn't dating her on the rebound.

They continued to see each other, and eventually Benny asked Miriam if she would marry him. She loved him, but she already had one failed marriage in her past, and she didn't want another so she was slow to commit. The problem, however, was his children. They seemed to like her, but they were still hoping Benny would get back together with their mother.

In addition, Benny's teenage daughter was a big problem. She lived with Benny most of the time, and he had never been much on disciplining his children. His ex-wife had given up on their daughter years ago. To Miriam, Benny's daughter was a big red flag, and she wasn't sure she could handle having the girl in her life. In the end, Miriam took the red flag as a real warning and stopped seeing Benny.

Then Miriam met Walter. He was a great guy, and he had a teenage daughter as well. Although not as wild as Benny's daughter, Walter's daughter needed a mother and welcomed Miriam with open arms, which made all the difference in Miriam and Walter's relationship. It was much easier to be a couple when they weren't always wondering what his daughter was up to.

Walter's daughter was happy for her father and Miriam to be a couple. In fact, she was the maid of honor at their wedding.

Everything was going great, and then Miriam got pregnant. All of a sudden, the three of them were going to be four, and Walter's daughter wondered if that would mean Miriam would love her less. Maybe her father would love her less, too. She'd never had to compete for her father's attention with a sibling before. What if they had a girl? Would she have to share her room with her new sister?

Any time there are changes in the family—whether it's a new baby, a relative temporarily living in the house, a grandparent moving in, or a child leaving for college—all changes add stress to a marriage. Change rocks the boat, and if we're not careful, change will overturn the boat, too, leaving a couple to sink or swim.

Whatever the case, spouses have to maintain their focus and make sure they dedicate time for themselves as a couple. Family members, as well as the couple, have to give space and grace to the marriage.

Who Do You Love More?

When Amy was five, she asked her father whom he loved the most, her mother or her. Amy's question put her father in a difficult position. He knew that if he said

"Mommy" it might hurt Amy's feelings; but if he said "Amy" and his wife found out, that wouldn't be good, either. So instead he mumbled something and left the room, but Amy wouldn't be put off so she went and asked her mother a similar question.

"Who do you love more, Daddy or me?"

Amy's mother took her into her arms and gave her a big hug. "Honey, you know I love you. I love you more than any other little girl in the world, and I love Daddy more than any other daddy in the world."

Amy's mother thought she had given a pretty clever answer, but Amy wasn't satisfied. She knew a dodge when she heard one. It didn't matter, though, because Amy knew her mother loved her best.

Who do you love more, your children or your spouse? That can be a difficult question to answer. Many experts say that, clearly, you love your spouse best. However, sometimes we don't act like it.

Sometimes it seems easier for you to love a child when your spouse is distant or when things are difficult for you as a couple. Other times, you love your spouse more because your child is being impossible.

Love just isn't something you can measure. In fact, the more love you have in your heart, the more love multiplies. It's not a matter of loving your children 25 percent and your spouse the other 75 percent. In any given situation, you have to love them both 100 percent. It's not a question of love, but it can be an issue of loyalty and who demands the most attention. However, in reality, you shouldn't love your spouse or your children first. First, you should love God.

Love God First

Jesus doesn't tell us how much to love other people, only to love God first and others as we love ourselves. As Christians, we know we are supposed to love God first. God is our priority as an individual, as a couple, and as a family. All else follows from that.

One night, George had a vivid dream, the kind he didn't have often. In the dream, George heard God call to him. Shocked to hear God's voice, George turned to look and see where the voice was coming from. It was coming from somewhere, but he couldn't figure out where.

God called to George again. "George!"

George said the only words that came to mind, the words of Samuel in the Bible: "Speak, Lord, for your servant is listening."

Even in his dream, George was surprised that those words came out. God then told him, "Go get your wife, your children, and all your worldly goods."

So George lined up everything he had—his wife, his children, his house, his job, and even his favorite boat.

Then God said, "Good. Now give them all to me."

This terrified George. It was especially difficult to hand over his daughter. She had been so ill recently that he was afraid to let her go, but slowly he took everyone and everything and gave them to God.

Then George felt God's eyes burn into him. "Now I'm giving all these things back to you; but remember that they are all mine, not yours. Your job is just to take care of them for me. Don't ever forget it."

Then George woke up in a cold sweat. He knew what God was trying to teach him. The people and things in his life, even his wife and children, were precious gifts from God. They were not his to treat casually as he wished. They were his to take care of for God, and George didn't forget it.

Later, when George told his wife about his dream, she just smiled. Then she took his hand and brought him back to bed. Space and grace.

After God, Your Spouse Comes First

I strongly believe that first things should always be first, no matter what type of marriage you are in, whether it is a traditional family or a blended family. If you are in a traditional family, it goes without saying that your mate should be your primary love focus. After all, there would be no children if the two of you had not formed some type of romantic, loving relationship.

However, even as it relates to blended families, your love for each other is still primary, even if your relationship happens after having children. Children ultimately take their cues and leadership from their parents.

While it may take a little while to happen, children's happiness and feelings of security are sparked by the happiness and feelings of security of their parents, especially if that particular parent has lived a miserable existence prior to this relationship. Children just want to know that this is going to be a long, lasting relationship and that they won't be left behind or alone.

Loving your mate sets the context for loving everyone else. There is no doubt that you love your spouse, but love means different things to different people; and much of what we think love is and how we show it depends on what happened to us while we were growing up.

Shelbie grew up in a home where love meant obeying her parents. There wasn't a lot of hugging, kissing, or other signs of affection. According to her parents, love meant that she showed them respect and honored their wishes.

One day, when Shelbie was in her late teens, she came home from school after a terrible day. She didn't want to talk about it, but she thought it would make her feel so much better if she could have a hug from her mother.

After dinner was over and the dishes were put away, Shelbie and her mother were alone in the kitchen. Shelbie poured out her heart about what had happened that day at school. As she talked she tried to draw closer to her mother. It would have been so easy for her mother to reach out and hold her and show her physical affection. Instead, her mother simply said, "I'm sorry, dear, but sometimes things like that happen." Then she walked away.

At first, Shelbie was crushed, but then she became angry. What was so wrong with giving a simple hug? Disappointed but forgiving, Shelbie knew it wasn't the way her mother showed love. *But still . . .* , she thought to herself.

Jamal grew up in a house that was always full of aunts, uncles, cousins, and friends—everyone was welcome. His mother and grandmother were great cooks, which was a good thing because they usually fed half the neighborhood.

After dinner, Jamal's mother hugged everyone, thanked them for coming, hugged them again, and then sent them home with a sack of leftovers. She also always hugged and kissed Jamal, which embarrassed him to no end.

Shelbie and Jamal started dating; and while she felt comfortable with the affection displayed at his house, he was just as happy to be left alone when he was at her house. They committed to each other and went on to have a bigger and better marriage. Then they had a baby boy.

Shelbie wanted her son to be the best little boy ever, but her way of showing love was to encourage him from afar. She didn't think it was good to cuddle him; it might make him soft.

On the other hand, Jamal couldn't understand why Shelbie wasn't "loving on" their son. She seemed cool and distant. In addition, she wasn't showing Jamal much physical attention, either. All she wanted to do was talk and have "meaningful" conversation. He had too much of that at work. When he was at home with his wife, he just wanted to hold her and make love.

Finally, Jamal and Shelbie's once rock-solid marriage started slip-sliding away, and they were headed toward divorce. In a last ditch effort to save their marriage, they went to a counselor who helped them understand what was happening.

The couple still loved each other and their son, but each needed to give the other space and grace. Jamal and Shelbie needed to do more than merely understand; they needed to behave toward each other with compassion and mercy. After receiving this wise counsel just in time, they were able to make their marriage bigger and better.

Marriage is not "once saved, always saved." Your marriage relationship can always backslide if you're not paying attention or if you let other things get in the way. That's why your relationship with your spouse is the most important thing after God, and learning how to love each other is a continual process that can bring you closer together.

A healthy couple is also more likely to have healthy children. A counselor friend told me that not long ago a desperate couple brought in their eight-year-old daughter for counseling. They said that everything was fine in the family expect for this one child who was always depressed. They thought perhaps she had a "chemical imbalance," or maybe she was too sensitive and let things bother her too much.

The parents had first gone to their pediatrician who thought the child was too young for depression medication and urged them to see my friend the counselor. At first, the parents assumed they would just drop off their daughter and return when her session was over. They didn't think they would need to stay, but the counselor asked them to remain in the room for the first visit.

As the counselor talked to the little girl, she noticed how the girl smiled. She was friendly but shy. However, the counselor noticed that as soon as the father started talking, the girl became anxious. When the two parents talked to each other, the girl became still and started looking at the door, like she wanted to run away and hide.

At the next session, the counselor met with the child alone. Again, the child was playful, and they had a great time making pictures with colored pencils. When the session was over and the parents came to pick up their daughter, the counselor again noticed how the child's behavior changed. The counselor thought all of this was strange.

The counselor's office window overlooked the parking lot, and as she watched the family leave, she saw something that gave her more insight about the child's behavior. The mother strapped her daughter into her car seat, and as she did, the father yelled at the mother. As an argument raged between the parents, the counselor caught a glimpse of the little girl's face. It all made sense now.

If you want a happy, well-adjusted child,
take care of yourself and your marriage.

When the parents brought the little girl for her next session, the counselor requested to meet with them without their daughter. *Finally*, the parents thought. *Maybe she'll tell us what's wrong with our little girl.*

After the parents were seated, the counselor asked a surprising question: "Are you planning to get a divorce?"

The parents flushed with shame.

"What makes you ask that?" the father asked.

"Just a good hunch," the counselor said. "But it's true, right?"

"Yes," the mother said. "Our marriage hasn't been right for a long time, and we've decided to call it quits."

"We'd never say anything to the kids, though. We don't want them to worry," added the father.

"Well, that's what's wrong with your daughter," the counselor said.

"How could our daughter possibly know?" both parents asked in unison.

The counselor explained: "Some people—and your daughter is one such person—are what we call empathic. They pick up on feelings that others miss. In a way, they act as a barometer for what's going on in the family. Your daughter knows something is wrong between the two of you, so if you want her to get better, get help for your marriage. You feel sad about the state of your marriage, right?"

"Yes," they replied.

"Your daughter is picking up on those feelings and reflecting them back to you through her behavior," the counselor said.

A family is more than the sum of individuals; a family is a system. The feelings and behavior of one member affect all the others. In this case, the child was expressing the feelings of the family system, which was sadness. She was like the canary in the coal mine. She could sense when no one else could that the oxygen was going out of the family in the form of a dysfunctional marriage relationship between her parents.

When the marriage got back on track, so did the little girl. She never had been the problem, but she had called attention to the problem in the only way she knew how. If you want healthy children, keep your marriage healthy.

My counselor friend said that another mother brought in her eighteen-month-old for counseling. She wasn't sure what the mother thought the problem was, but it wasn't the toddler.

When the counselor probed a little bit about what was going on with the mother, the mother became angry—a little too angry given the circumstance. So the counselor advised the woman to take care of herself and whatever issues she had, and her child would have a much better chance of being better, too. When you get your relational priorities straight, some—though not all—of your problems will fall into place.

Once you and your spouse start having children, it can become more difficult for you to find time alone. Here are some things Vanessa and I do: We make perpetual dating a priority. The last 21 years of marriage have included blending our two sons and adopting our daughter along with the arrival of our grandchildren, but our dating philosophy remains the same: "By any means necessary!" Simply put, we understand that where there is a will, there is a way, so we find a way! Remember, losers make excuses while winners make a way.

Another thing that might be helpful is to plan ahead and incorporate "village" support for those occasions when you need personal time with each other. There is a lot of truth to the saying "It takes a village to raise a child." To make those times just for us, Vanessa and I also remained aware of the fact that while we may not always be able to control quantity of time, we could control quality of time.

Love Your Children

It probably seems obvious that parents should love their children, but ask yourself, *How much time do I spend with my children?* Studies show that parents spend more time driving to work than they spend with their children each day. We all have limits to our time and energy, but there are some things you can do.

- Carve out time to be alone with each child, even if it's reading a bedtime story.
- Have a daily routine where you ask each child three things: what they learned, what kindness they showed, and what they're grateful for. If you get into a habit of asking these three questions, it won't be long before your children anticipate what you're going to ask, and they will have their answers ready.
- Eat together as a family as often as possible but without the TV on or cell phones at the table. Pray before the meal, share family stories, and tell jokes.
- Set a time every month or so for a family outing or activity. You can watch a movie, play music

together, or watch a TV show. You don't have to spend money. The most important thing is to spend time together. Talk to one another. Get to know one another.

- Most Sundays, Vanessa and I have brunch with our children and grandchildren. It dawned on me that I know exactly what time church convenes each week, without exception, but I didn't have an established time to be with my family. Based on Scripture, the institution of family begins in Genesis, while the church does not come into being until Acts, which means God created family long before he established the church. So why does the church (which is secondary) have an established day and time, while my family (which is primary) has to be satisfied with wherever we can fit in and has no established day or time? That didn't sound right to us, so we fixed it: Family first; church second.

Extended Family Issues

With children comes lots of advice from extended family members, but not all of it is helpful. Sarah and Evan's baby was the first grandchild in their families, so not only did they become parents, but there were now grandmothers, grandfathers, great-aunts, and so on.

When children enter the picture, people step into new roles and titles, and believe me, some grandparents take seriously being Grams, Pop, or whatever name they're called. I knew one grandmother who thought she was too young to be called Grandmother, so she decided the baby would call her Mimi.

Just as other family members may have an opinion about what they want to be called, they may also have an opinion about how you should raise your children. We'll deal more with that subject in another chapter; but it's important to remember that the parents are the parents, and they are the ones who are primarily responsible for their children.

For example, Sarah and Evan were visiting Evan's parents, and his father said, "Now, I don't want to hear that baby cry." It was the baby's nap time, and Sarah and Evan were trying to get him to sleep without rocking him for hours. Although they agreed not to let the baby cry too much, they knew they might have to let him cry some before he finally drifted off to sleep.

Sarah and Evan weren't being mean to their baby; they just wanted him to learn that he'd be OK if they laid him in his crib. However, Evan's father had his own opinion about how they should get the baby to sleep. He thought their way was a terrible idea. He said, "No baby will ever cry in my house."

What should Sarah and Evan have done? Sarah wanted Evan to stand up to his father, but Evan was a new father and thought maybe babies shouldn't be left to cry. Sarah told Evan that if they were ever going to have time alone together, the baby had to learn to go to sleep on his own.

Evan decided he couldn't tell his father to mind his own business, so they didn't bring the baby over very often, which confused the grandparents. Sarah would have been only too happy to tell them, but Evan put his foot down. By not supporting his wife and choosing his parents over her, he caused their bigger and better marriage to slip.

Here are some things we've found that will help you keep your family from interfering with your role as parents.

1. Establish and write down your parenting philosophy.
2. Be willing to put space between you and those who refuse to comply with your philosophy.
3. Explain the reasons for your philosophy to the family.
4. Never allow family members to undermine the rules you have established as a couple.
5. Express to your parents that while you are their child, their grandchildren are your children, and you and your mate have the last word.

Take Away

Having children transitions a couple into a family, which changes everything. However, with thoughtful actions and by sticking to your mission, you can go on to the next level and have a bigger and better marriage full of grace and space.

Sharing Space and Grace

1. What's the best thing about being a parent? What's the worst thing?

2. In your home, who disciplines the children? What is your philosophy about discipline? How do your thoughts about discipline differ, if any, from your parents?

3. What are some things you plan to do differently from your parents? Why?

4. Write a list of ten things you want your children to learn from you.

5. Write a list of ten things your children have taught you about being a parent.

CHAPTER FIVE

WHEN A BIGGER AND BETTER MARRIAGE BECOMES AN EMPTY NEST

But they that wait upon the LORD shall renew their strength; they shall mount up with wings as eagles; they shall run, and not be weary; and they shall walk, and not faint.

—Isaiah 40:31, KJV

WHEN A BIGGER AND BETTER MARRIAGE BECOMES AN EMPTY NEST

We say that when all the eaglets have flown the nest never to return, the couple's home becomes an empty nest and the parents become empty-nesters. However, sometimes this transition from having children at home to not having them at home doesn't go smoothly, which can knock even a bigger and better marriage off its foundation.

Some couples look forward to becoming empty-nesters the day their children are born. Zulema loved to sleep late on Saturday mornings. She figured she worked hard all week, and Saturday was her time to relax. This routine continued when Zulema and Andy married. Saturday morning was their time.

The Saturday after Zulema learned she was pregnant, she looked up at the ceiling from her cozy bed and thought, *I won't get to do this again until all the kids are gone.* She was right.

It didn't matter what day it was, the baby woke up at 5 A.M. Then there were two boys; and after they started playing

Little League, Saturday became the day when Zulema had to get up early and get them to practice. Even when there was no Saturday practice, it didn't matter because Andy had hired a pitching coach for one-on-one practice for the boys.

Andy worked most Saturdays, so the burden was all on Zulema. She was right that she wouldn't get her Saturdays back until after the children left home. She loved her children but looked forward to having more time for herself after they were on their own.

When the Eaglets Won't Leave the Nest

In preparation to house their baby birds, eagles often feather their nests with moss, leaves, and mud to make it as soft and warm as possible. However, when it's time for the eaglets to be independent, the mother eagle and the father eagle stir up the nest so the eaglets will want to leave.

Once the nest is stirred, the little sticks that hadn't been allowed to poke through are now forced through the soft moss and the leaves. The nest becomes prickly and uncomfortable to live in.

Some children don't, can't, or won't leave home. They've grown comfortable in their parents' safe and loving care. There are few stresses, worries, or responsibilities there, so they decide to stay long past the time when they should be independent. Sometimes as parents, we have to stir up the nest so our children will leave and begin their own lives.

As a couple, you need to decide when it's time for your children to leave home. You and your spouse may have sharp differences of opinion on this matter; but be aware, your expectations are shaped to some degree by your own opinion as well as your family-of-origin's experience.

From the time he could remember, Ben's parents had told him that once he graduated from high school, he would be out on his own. So on his eighteenth birthday, his friends helped him move into a condo.

When Ben had children of his own, he expected the same from them. After all, he'd made it all right when he left home. They would, too. However, his wife grew up differently. In her house, children were expected to go to college and get a job after graduation. Her parents didn't expect her to move out until she was twenty-one and had a job. It was fine with them if she lived at home until then.

With their children, Ben's wife was fine with them staying at home past high school. A conflict between Ben and his wife followed about when it would be the "right" time for their children to leave home.

Having no children at home can give you time
to get reacquainted with each other.

After Jane graduated from college, she planned to go on to graduate school. She was more than ready to leave home. In fact, she couldn't leave soon enough.

When discussing her plans with her parents, though, Jane was shocked by her father's response. When she told them that she thought she'd find an apartment because the university didn't have graduate school housing, her father became angry.

"Why do you want to go to school close by but not live at home?" he asked.

Jane was incredulous. "Why would anyone live with their parents after college?"

Her response made her father even angrier. He told her that if that was the way she felt, she could leave immediately.

After things settled down, Jane's parents had a long conversation. Her mother encouraged Jane to move out on her own because she remembered when she herself was in her twenties. Her mother told her that after she had graduated from high school, she had left home and had found a job in New York City. Those were some of the best times of her life. She couldn't deny her daughter that same experience.

Then her mother reminded Jane's father what it was like when he came home from the Army and had to live under his parents' roof as an adult.

"But I did it," Jane's father said.

"Yes, you did, but you ended up hating your parents."

"Yes, but Jane's a girl. I was a soldier."

Different expectations, different family histories, different times.

Olivia's parents were great. They created such a loving environment in their home that it became the place where all of Olivia's friends hung out. While high school was difficult for a lot of teens, she loved every minute of it.

Olivia's parent's made sure she had the best they could provide. Because she was in the band, which demanded so much time during the summer, she never had a summer job like many other teens, so she didn't have to scramble to save money for the things she needed.

Since Olivia's childhood was such smooth sailing, when it was time for her to assume adult responsibilities, she didn't have a lot of experience. After college, she returned home, not because she wanted to but because she had nowhere else to go. Finally, she found a teaching job and saved enough money for her own place, but her parents invited her to continue to live with them so she could save her money and eventually buy a house sometime in the future.

The relationship Olivia had with her parents was of such that she could be independent and still live with them. Neither lifestyle conflicted. She was responsible and tried not to worry her parents by staying out all hours, and her parents insisted that she needed to do her share of the cooking and cleaning. It all worked out for everyone.

Melba was a different story. As parents, part of our job is to help prepare our children to live independently. We often talk about preparing them to launch into the world, but sometimes the launch doesn't go according to plan.

Melba always had a tough time making good decisions. In fact, it was difficult for her to settle on anything for long, so she didn't do much for a couple of years after high school because she couldn't decide where she wanted to go or what she wanted to do. While her friends were getting on with their lives, she seemed stuck.

When she finally decided on a career path, Melba enrolled in a local college. Going to a local school was appealing because she could live at home where her mother did everything for her just as she always had, and her father continued paying for her car and her gas.

When Melba again changed her mind about her career, she transferred to a different college. Finally, after seven years she graduated, but she couldn't find a job. She continued to live at home, and her parents kept taking care of her as they always had.

After several months, Melba stopped even looking for a job, but her parents made a decision. It was time to stir up the nest. They gave her a date when she had to have a job and be out of their house. Melba was surprised but didn't do anything about it.

After the deadline passed, Melba came home one evening after being out with her friends to find that her door key did not work. Then she saw several bags and suitcases next to the door with a note that read, "Melba, we love you, but it's time to grow up. Call us when you find your own place. Love, Mom and Dad." *That* is stirring up the nest.

Perhaps you don't need to go to this extreme and change the locks, but a bigger and better marriage should accommodate eaglets only for so long. Part of your job as a parent is to make sure your children are independent, responsible adults. When that happens, you've done your job, and now it's time for them to do theirs because there is a lot more living to do as a couple after the children are gone.

On Again, Off Again Empty-Nesters

What if your children leave and come back? It's up to you as a couple to decide what do, but be aware how your own past affects your decisions.

While it will be hard for some children to adjust to life out in the real world—with the current job market and the difficulties for even well-qualified people to find a job— these days it can be even more difficult for young adults to have the financial resources to have their own place. Many parents find that their children leave home and then come back, and sometimes they come back with a partner and maybe with children of their own.

Joanne's husband was deployed again, so this time she decided that it might be best to take the children and go back to her parents' house until he was stateside again. Her parents were happy to spend more time with Joanne and her three children, but they weren't prepared for having preschoolers in the house again.

Even though the children were well behaved, the twin boys were still only two years old, and their sister was just four. In others words, even the best behaved two- and four-year-olds need a childproof home, and the grandparents scrambled to get breakables put up as high as possible.

It's not that the grandparents didn't love Joanne and the children, but they thought their days of caring for children were long gone. Surprise! They weren't.

When Joanne and her children were finally settled in with her parents, it was clear that she was exhausted. Those twins were a handful, so Grandma did her best to ease her daughter's stress by doing what she'd always done—cook, clean, and pick up.

Another change for Joanne's parents involved their social life. Both of them were retired, so they had settled into a comfortable routine of hosting their friends at their house. However, they could no longer host their weekly bridge game. Having a house full of people would disturb the children's bedtime routine, and Joanne wanted the children in bed by 8:30, so anything that might interfere with that was forbidden.

Joanne's parents didn't mind not hosting the bridge game. They decided they could always go to someone else's house. If that were the only disruption to their lives it wouldn't have been so bad, but they were starting to see that their home life was now in flux.

With no children to look after for the past several years, Joanne's parents didn't usually eat a big dinner. But after the children arrived, even their meals required more time and preparation, and clean-up left the grandparents more tired than they had been in years.

When their son-in-law came home from overseas, Joanne moved back on base. After all the adjustments they had had to make, her parents rested for a solid week. They were relieved and more than ready to go back to being empty-nesters.

You may be getting used to being a couple again and enjoying the freedom. A colleague told me that now that her children are gone, she is so relieved she doesn't have to fix "instant" dinner anymore. You know that meal you have to throw together in no time because your children have to be somewhere else in ten minutes. Having no children in the house allows you to be back in control of your own schedule.

Empty Feelings After the Nest Becomes Empty

While there are good things about having no children in the house, there are things you might miss. A mother I know missed having her daughter around. Her daughter had just landed her first job and had moved to another state. Her husband had a demanding job and worked long hours. The house felt so empty, and she found herself alone most of the time.

Those were the times she missed her daughter most, even though when her daughter had lived at home she was constantly talking on the phone or was preoccupied with her friends much of the time. Now all the mother had was a TV, which she kept on for noise.

An empty nest can be an opportunity
for new adventures and reinvention.

After a few weeks of moping around, the mother realized that she needed her life back, so she started volunteering at church and inviting friends for lunch. She even thought about getting a part-time job.

Getting Reacquainted

When children move out or away, couples sometimes find that they need to spend more time together. Having time for "us" is a chance for a couple to get reacquainted and fall deeper in love.

Suzy and Harry had just married off their last child. They were alone for the first time in thirty years. One day, Suzy looked at Harry and asked, "When did you get those gray hairs?" Then she smiled at her own gray hairs and laughed. "I think I'll go to the beauty shop and get some highlights."

Becoming a couple again and getting reacquainted gives you a chance to do new things for yourself and for each other. Suzy and Harry started taking ballroom dancing lessons and meeting new friends.

Making New Friends

After the children are gone, it can be challenging to make new friends. It's easy when you have little ones because babies naturally attract attention. New mothers seem to find one another in their neighborhood or through online meet-and-greets. They have a lot in common; they have the children in common and everything that goes with being mothers.

When young families show up at church, they are greeted with enthusiasm. It means the church is growing and attracting a younger crowd, and that's always good. Even when you talk to co-workers, many times you share stories about your children. Having children means you always have funny or tragic stories to tell.

However, when your children are gone, it can be harder to meet new people. If you move to a new community, it can be like everyone already has their friends. It can be difficult to break into a new crowd, which can also be disappointing given that now you have more time and hopefully more money to play with.

Think about how many new places you had to go because of your children. Maybe you met parents at karate class, at dance, at school, on the ball field, in the nursery at church, at the skating rink, at daycare, at scouts—and the list goes on. But even though it can be tough to meet new people, it's worth a try.

Maybe you're too shy to put yourself out and start meeting new people and making new friends, or maybe you're happy with the friends you have. The point is that being an empty-nester can be a time to try new and different things.

A bigger and better marriage is always growing and changing, and without children you can give your spouse more space and grace. You don't have to keep doing things the way you've always done them.

Here are some things that changed for Vanessa and me after the children were out of the house. They are new and different ways we found space and grace for each other.

1. We adjusted to the fact that because the children were gone, everyone left in the house was an equal.
2. We started making plans as partners and not as parents.
3. We gave ourselves permission to be a couple again and selfishly take time to get to know each other all over again. Getting reacquainted means that you might find that wild and crazy guy or girl you married. Being an empty-nester can give you the opportunity to find new wild and crazy things to do together.

Reinvent Yourselves as a Couple

Being empty-nesters can be a time for you to reinvent yourselves as a couple. It can be a time to try new things. Perhaps you want to start your own business. Maybe you want to take a few classes at a local community center or college.

It used to be said that people in their fifties and sixties were old, but that's no longer the case. Years ago, the government made sixty-five the retirement age because at that time people didn't live much longer than that. Life expectancy was shorter. Now, with the possibility of longer and healthier lives, you might live another forty-plus years after retirement. That's almost another entire lifetime.

Don't waste this good gift from God. Take this opportunity and try something new. Revisit postponed goals and dreams. Use the time you need in the past for parental chores and create plans that will occupy you as a couple.

Beware: Someone Else Might

As I mentioned, being an empty-nester means you get another chance to fall deeper in love with your spouse. But what if things have shifted? Things shift, and people change. That's to be expected.

What if you find that you've grown apart? Once the children are gone, what if you have nothing to talk about with your spouse? Being a parent can be a consuming job, but you must be careful not to lose touch with your spouse or let your children push you apart.

When the children were all married with children of their own, Laura decided she wanted to take up painting again. With the children at home, she never had the time, but now some of her unfulfilled dreams resurfaced. She loved painting so much. Why had she ever let it go?

Her husband, Clive, had no use for any of that art stuff. To him it was a waste of time. Besides, what would she do with all those pictures once she painted them? She could hang only so many in their house, and surely their friends and the children wouldn't want them. He needed to give Laura space and grace.

For Clive, one thing was for sure, with the children gone, he could watch basketball all day with no interruptions if he wanted to. Laura saw no point in watching basketball. She didn't know any of the players and couldn't care less about the sport. She needed to give Clive space and grace. They both needed to give each other space and grace because if they didn't, someone else might.

There was an attractive man at the place where Laura took art lessons. In her opinion, he was paying a little too much attention to her. Then one day, he asked if she'd like to go for coffee.

He's trying to pick me up! Laura thought. "Sorry, I'm flattered, but I'm also happily married," she told him.

Laura got in her car to leave, but she couldn't help thinking to herself, *It would have been so easy for me to go out with that man. If that's the case, am I happily married?*

When she got home, Laura gave Clive a big kiss. Even though he was taken by surprise, he liked her spontaneous kiss and reciprocated. Yes, they were happily married. In that moment, Laura found the grace to watch basketball more often with Clive; and Clive thought that if Laura's painting classes made her that exuberant, then he was happy for her to take all the classes she wanted.

No matter how long you've been married and no matter how much you love each other, if you're not growing as a couple, your marriage is slipping. Bert was the CEO of a small firm, and he traveled a lot for work. Recently, he hired a new assistant. She was a lovely married woman with a son away at school, so she was free to accompany Bert on his business trips. Most of the time, he was oblivious to her. To him, she was just his assistant—nothing more.

Then one day, Bert's wife, Sheila, met him at his office for lunch. Bert may not have noticed how his assistant paid attention to him, but Sheila did. To her it was clear that the assistant had her eye on Bert.

Later that evening, Sheila casually mentioned to her husband her observation about his assistant. He just laughed it off. He thought his wife was jealous for no reason. He prided himself on being able to read people. He didn't think his assistant had any designs on him. *That's just silly!* he thought.

Bert's next business trip was scheduled for the following week, and his assistant asked to go with him. He thought about it and decided that maybe it was a good idea because she could do the contract paperwork there. Because he thought Sheila would pitch a fit, he didn't tell her his assistant was going. *Besides*, he thought, *there isn't anything to tell. It is business as usual.*

The first night at the hotel, Bert asked his assistant if she would join him for dinner. They were seated in a booth, and after they had had a few drinks he noticed that his assistant was sitting uncomfortably close. As much as he hated to admit it, maybe his wife wasn't completely off base.

Bert excused himself, saying that he needed to make a call and would have to call it a night. He paid the check and almost ran to his room. He felt guilty for not telling his wife that his assistant was going on the trip with him. If she found out, she might think he set the whole thing up.

Bert was so bothered that he cut his meetings short the next day and caught an early flight home. When he walked in, Sheila had just gotten home from work herself. Surprised, she asked, "Why are you home so early? Is everything all right?"

Bert dropped his briefcase and took her hand. "Boy, I'm glad I'm married to you!"

Sheila knew something was up. While Bert thought he could read people, Sheila thought he was an open book.

She had her suspicions about what had happened but didn't say anything. *Let him stew*, she thought.

A few days later, Sheila brought up Bert's trip.

"OK, you can tell me. What happened?"

Bert let it all out—how Sheila had been right about his assistant. With that, Sheila could have said "I told you so," but she gave Bert space and grace.

"What are you going to do about it?" Sheila asked.

"She's got to go," Bert said. He was grateful for his wife's understanding, but he pressed on.

"I was blind," he said. "Maybe I gave her some unconscious sign that I was interested in her or that I was looking for someone outside my marriage." Then Bert had an idea. "Let's book a vacation, and if you can get time off from work, you can come with me on the next business trip."

Sheila decided that it didn't matter what her boss said. She was going!

If you're not paying attention to your spouse, someone else might be watching and waiting for a chance to wreck your marriage.

Take Away

Once the eaglets are gone, it can be your opportunity as a couple to rebuild your nest or even to move to another mountaintop and build there. A bigger and better marriage continues to grow and change, even after the children have left home. Remember, no two things can occupy the same space at the same time, and grace is better when shared.

Offering Space and Grace

1. What is one thing you look forward to about being an empty-nester?

2. Describe what you'd like your relationship to be with your adult children.

3. What are your ground rules for children who return home alone or with friends and families of their own?

4. When is the time to offer advice, and when is the time to keep quiet?

5. Share a time when you offered advice to your adult children. What happened as a result?

6. What's the best way to help your children now that they are adults?

CHAPTER SIX

A BIGGER AND BETTER MARRIAGE IN YOUR GOLDEN YEARS

For which cause we faint not; but though our outward man perish, yet the inward man is renewed day by day. For our light affliction, which is but for a moment, worketh for us a far more exceeding and eternal weight of glory; while we look not at the things which are seen, but at the things which are not seen: for the things which are seen are temporal; but the things which are not seen are eternal.

—1 Corinthians 4:16-18, KJV

A BIGGER AND BETTER MARRIAGE IN YOUR GOLDEN YEARS

Not Like They Used to Be

When we used to talk about people in their golden years, we were talking about people who were riding off into the sunset. They were headed out to pasture; they were ready for a life of ease and comfort.

That's what an elderly woman in one of my congregations thought. After her husband died, Agnes said, "No more cooking. No more house chores. I'm going to live with my daughter and let her do the work. I've worked my whole life, and I've earned the right to take it easy in my last remaining years."

Be golden in your golden years
because the best is yet to come.

Agnes moved in with her daughter and quit doing anything, but that didn't last long. After a visit to the doctor, he assured her that she was as healthy as a horse, and there was no reason she couldn't live another twenty years.

Agnes told her daughter afterward, "Don't get me wrong, but twenty years is a long time. While I like being waited on, it's not fair to you or to the rest of the family. I think it's time I went back to being productive."

Growing up in her family, Agnes always thought that her great-grandparents and even her parents had one foot in the grave, or so it had appeared to her. That's what she expected when she entered her golden years; but now that she was the great-grandmother, she had no intention of getting anywhere close to a cemetery.

Our golden years are not like they used to be. More and more elderly people hold jobs, and the fastest growing segment of the population includes people over 100 years old.

An organist I once knew retired and moved to another state to be closer to her children. She was doing all right financially, but she decided a little pocket cash would help, so she found a local church and presented herself as their new organist. Her arrival was perfectly timed because the church was looking to replace the organist they had. She played for the church's two services each Sunday, as well as for any extra services, including weddings.

After several years, now well into her seventies, the organist decided to switch things up a bit. She got a job playing the organ at a church in another denomination. I think she finally retired when her playing didn't satisfy her anymore—when she was nearing ninety!

This woman was still high-spirited and even left detailed directions for the musicians who played at her funeral. Believe me, she went out to pasture kicking and screaming.

Today's Golden Years

Times are long gone when many people retire with a company pension. Lucy had worked as a seamstress in a laundry for over forty years. When she retired thirty years ago, she had enough to live comfortably in her own home.

Back then it was not uncommon for men, especially, to die shortly after they retired, not because of illness but because they didn't see the point of living with nothing to do. Their lives were so defined by what they did rather than who they were that once they left work, they just faded away.

Today, things are better and worse. These days we're pretty much on our own.

True, there is Social Security and Medicare, but more seniors find that they need a job to make ends meet. Some Baby Boomers have no plans to ever retire because they can't afford to or they think the prospect of retiring and having so much time on their hands is unappealing.

However, your golden years can be a time to reinvent yourself. You can pursue new hobbies, meet new people, and do interesting things with your spouse to make your marriage bigger and better.

Perhaps you have a bucket list. A bucket list contains all of things you've always wanted to do—the things you want to do before you die. You can also have a bucket list as a couple.

Here are some of the things Vanessa and I plan to do:

1. Write more books together as well as individually.
2. Travel and do things such as eat pasta in Italy, go on a date in Paris, and see the Seven Wonders of the World.
3. Learn to speak other languages.
4. Become philanthropists.
5. Be completely debt-free by age sixty-five.
7. Spend Christmas in New York with our children and grandchildren.
8. Make a large donation to pancreatic and breast cancer foundations in honor of our mothers.

New Times, New Standards for Parents

Have you ever looked at your parents' high school yearbooks? It can be hard to imagine that they were ever young. Perhaps you've been at a family reunion where someone posted old pictures of your relatives. I once saw a picture of one of my grandparents. I thought she looked so old. Then I figured out how old she was when the picture was taken, and I was surprised to learn that she was younger than I am now!

Age is a matter of perspective. I'm sure you've noticed that people your own age don't look particularly old, and people in their thirties look like babies. OK, maybe that is a slight exaggeration, but I think you know what I mean.

When I was twenty, I felt quite grown up. Actually, I felt grown up when I was a lot younger than that. I knew I didn't know all there was to know, but I thought I knew enough to more than get by.

You often hear people say they wish they could turn back the clock but keep all the things they've learned. Most people think that way, sometimes including me. So I try to keep this in mind when it comes to dealing with younger parents. They may look young to me, but I look old to them; and in their minds, they are seasoned adults.

If you've successfully launched your children and they are on their own, they need to make their own decisions without interference. I knew a man who insisted on buying American-made cars. To him, buying a foreign car was akin to treason against this country. Despite his strong feelings, the first car his son bought was a Honda.

Although the son told his father that the car he bought was actually made in the United States, it didn't matter. To his father, buying that foreign car was a slap in the face to American auto workers.

As the argument heated up, the father kept saying, "Son, don't you know that Americans should drive American cars?" The son answered with compassion, "Dad, you don't know what you're talking about. It doesn't matter who owns the company. It's who does the job."

The father regarded himself as the authority on cars and believed that his son was too young to know any better. The father also thought his opinion should carry more weight. It didn't matter that the father was eighty and the son was sixty. Experience to make decisions is in the eye of the beholder.

Sometimes it's hard for us to see our children for the adults they are. This is especially true when it comes to being grandparents and dealing with your children as parents.

Jill and Martin were a young couple who had been married for five years before they decided to have children. Since they planned on having only one child, they wanted to do everything right, so they were careful and thoughtful and read every book they could on the subject of parenting.

When they thought they had learned enough, they started trying to get pregnant. To Martin's parents, this was all nonsense. Didn't they know that you can never know enough to be parents? There is no way that any book can tell you everything you need to know, they reasoned. But they respected what they saw as their children's inexperience and didn't say anything. *Let them find out,* they thought.

Jill's parents had always had a hard time seeing her as an adult. To Jill, it seemed they had treated her the same way since she was five years old. Indeed, her parents had robbed her of making her own decisions well into her adulthood, and they were always giving Jill and Martin unwanted "helpful advice." It had become so annoying that Jill didn't want to tell her parents about some of the decisions she and Martin had already made.

For example, one of the parenting books suggested co-sleeping. Several of Jill's friends had done it with great success. For those unfamiliar with co-sleeping, it is the practice of sleeping in the same bed with your infant or young child.

The thinking goes that co-sleeping helps with breast-feeding. Experts also say that it helps promote healthy bonding with the infant, to say nothing about not having to get up out of bed in the middle of the night to feed the baby.

Jill was certain that her parents would have an opinion, so she didn't want to tell them that she and Martin planned to keep the baby in bed with them. In fact, she wasn't sure she wanted her mother to help out at all after the baby was born. Jill thought it would be too stressful. However, she figured that her parents would find out eventually, so it was probably best to get the news out now.

Jill had also hired a midwife, something else her parents thought strange. As her parents discussed all these new, odd (to them), and perhaps dangerous ideas, they finally decided that Jill and Martin were the parents and would have to learn the hard way; but they still weren't overly impressed with Jill's decisions.

Before the baby came, Jill had a frank conversation with her mother. "Mom," she said, "I'm going to be the mom, and you're going to be the grandmother. I know that will be new to you, but do you want to be like Grandma Ruth?"

Jill's mother had to stop and think. Did she want to be like her mother-in-law—bossy, opinionated, constantly undermining her as a mother? Or did she want to be like her own mother—caring, wise, and supportive of her as a parent?

Jill's mother broke down and cried. "It's terrible to say, but I've been acting like Grandma Ruth, haven't I? OK, I don't understand anything about midwives or co-sleeping. Give me the information, and I'll learn more. But you know I tell you these things because I love you."

"Yes," said Jill, "but try not to love me so much."

When you think about it, we all know that what counts as good parenting changes over time. For example, in the early 1920's, babies were left in the cradle much of the time, and they were bundled up tightly as they slept.

In the 1950's, the new thing was to put babies on a feeding schedule. The thinking went that babies were like everybody else and needed to eat regularly—once but no more than every three to four hours—and babies slept in a crib with lots of blankets.

In the 1970's, things changed again. Breastfeeding was becoming "a thing," and it was thought that good parents let their babies set their own schedules. So babies could eat as often as they wanted. There were no more four-hour feeding schedules. Babies slept in a baby bed on their stomachs, if that was comfortable for them. After all, it was up to babies to decide how they wanted to sleep or when they wanted to eat.

In the twenty-first century, the standards of good parenting have changed yet again. It is probably good to have babies on feeding schedules; and babies, if they aren't co-sleeping, sleep on their backs with no blankets. Standards of what is considered appropriate discipline have also changed.

Years ago, my mother-in-law, being the loving grandmother she was, interfered when I chastised my young son. As a result, we had a discussion about our different roles—me as the father and her as the grandmother.

I reminded her that she had raised all girls and that part of my responsibility was to make sure my son would become a productive man. Not long ago, our daughter had a similar conversation with my wife concerning our own grandchildren.

Becoming a Grandparent

Here are ten tips for grandparenting:

1. Never forget that you are in a new role.
2. Never make your adult child a child in the eyes of their children.

3. Never break the rules your children have made for their children.

4. Always check with your children first before doing something with their children for the first time or doing something you've not first discussed with them.

5. Never voice your disagreement with your children in front of the grandchildren.

6. Always establish your house rules with the parents so they can convey them to the grandchildren.

7. Never say yes to something when the parents have already said no.

8. Never buy extravagant gifts without the parents' consent.

9. Never forget that your child still needs you to be their parents.

10. Never grow too old to change.

How we raise our children and the standards of what counts as good parenting continue to change. Things that were once considered "in" and "the thing to do" are now out of style or considered wrong. It shouldn't be a surprise, then, that grandparenting has changed, too.

I was surprised to learn that there are now showers for grandparents. I've heard it's a fun time, but I didn't know just how many books there were on the subject or that you can give a "Congratulations on Becoming a Grandparent" card.

I've even seen books such as *From Grandmother With Love*, by Becky Kelly. In these books, grandparents, not just the grandmother, can put in family photos and record important family events and stories. These books are meant as keepsakes for the grandchildren because so many families live in different parts of the country and not in the same neighborhood or close by. These books are a great way to hand down stories you consider important.

However, becoming a grandparent can make you feel like other people see you as old when you don't necessarily feel that way. Our culture worships youth, and getting old is almost considered a crime. It certainly makes it harder to get a job as you get older.

Have you noticed that past a certain age, young people may not talk to you anymore? I've heard older people say that it's like they're not even there when it comes to young people. It's not unusual for small children to be afraid of "old" people.

I didn't realize that children are sometimes afraid of old people because I never was. However, a friend told me that her children didn't want to hug or kiss their great-aunt when they went to see her. She said that her great-aunt told her that it was OK and not to push them because she'd been forced to hug old people when she was little.

Not all children are like this, of course. Some children seem to gravitate toward older people. But again, being old is often in the eye of the beholder.

Grandparents are special. They love their grandchildren perhaps in ways they couldn't love their own children.

John had never spent much time around babies, and that was all right with him. But when he became a parent, he was uncomfortable holding them when they cried or when they needed their diapers changed. In fact, he refused to change some diapers altogether.

John loved his children, but while they were growing up, he worked long hours in order to provide for his family. That meant he missed out on a lot of the day-to-day things that make up family life. When he became a grandfather, however, he decided things would be different. He and his grandson developed a close bond.

Of course, you've undoubtedly heard this from some grandparents. They can spoil their grandchildren and play with them all day and then send them home.

If your grandchildren don't live within driving distance and you have to stay in a hotel when you visit them, after having fun you can go back to the hotel and get a full night's sleep. Yes, there are advantages to being a grandparent.

In a humorous way, I believe that becoming a grandparent is also God's "revenge" for your children doing some of the things they did when they were little. My grandchildren have a Sunday ritual. They know that Papa (that's what they call me) keeps candy in a dish on his desk and that the candy is just for them. To me, one of the great joys of being a grandparent is to "sugar-up" my grandchildren and then send them home!

Please don't think that my lovely Vanessa is an angel when it comes to this, either. One of the things she does when she sees that the grandchildren are about to get in trouble is that she will "hide" them until their parents forget what they have done. It's so great being a grandparent!

However, you are more than grandparents or parents. You and your spouse are also a couple with your own priorities, your own lives. Psychologists say that we need to be self-differentiated. In simplest terms, being self-differentiated means that you are a separate individual. Your spouse is not you. This may sound obvious, but for some people who are overly dependent or controlling, it is not. Your character and success as a person doesn't depend on anyone but you.

Your children are their own persons, too. They have separate problems and have to make separate decisions. A family, like a couple, is not a blob of people melted into some kind of super-person. A family, like a couple, is made up of individuals who can come together to love and nurture one another but who are also free to have their own space and grace as separate people.

This applies to families who live under one roof, and it applies to extended family members of different generations. It can be tempting as grandparents to make up for things we did as parents at the expense of our children as parents or our grandchildren. Loving yourself and fulfilling your own dreams through your children and grandchildren is not love. It is selfish.

Family Griot

One role we play as grandparents in our golden years can be the family griot. *Griot* is a West African term. It's pronounced "jali" or "jeli." A griot is the repository of oral tradition, the stories. Traditionally, the griot is also a leader and an advisor sometimes to royalty. It is a position of honor and responsibility.

A grandparent is ideally suited to be a griot. He or she is someone who not only knows the family stories but who shares them with younger generations. As a couple, you together are griots. Your rock-solid marriage is a witness and a story for others to emulate. This is part of your legacy.

One of the things my wife and I strongly caution couples about is that many times as Christians, if we are not careful, we will place church before our families. That means that your children will know more about church than they know about their own family. They may even begin to feel as if, when compared to the church, they don't matter.

Based on Scripture, however, the family comes first. It trumps and even eclipses the importance of the church in terms of intimacy and sharing information.

Families should have times and occasions regularly set aside to tell family stories and even secrets. Having a special time set aside for the family means that all the family members can have assurance and take comfort that there is a dependable safe space where private information can be shared.

Being Golden

Alyce and Herb had been married for fifty years. They had been childhood sweethearts, and through good times and bad times they found a way to give space and grace to each other. While they had bumps along the way, their marriage was rock-solid.

When most adults were too busy talking to other adults, Herb always had a kind word for children—his and everybody else's. At church, children flocked to him because he always had a pocketful of candy, which he generously shared.

Alyce's face was kind and sweet. It was care-worn, but her loving Christian spirit shown through. I'm sure she got angry from time to time, but I never saw it. Neither she nor Herb had a bad word to say about anyone.

I hate to admit it, but I feared Herb and Alyce might be too good to be true. So one night after a meeting at church, I asked Stan, their son, if they were the same way at home as we saw them at church. Stan smiled and said, "Yes. They are truly golden."

Yes, the word *golden* described them exactly.

Conclusion

For almost twenty-two years, Vanessa and I have experienced an incredible marriage. To some on the outside, our marriage appears to be a beautiful fairytale. However, if the truth be told, the honest depiction of our marriage is about space and grace.

Our marriage has become bigger and better because of our willingness to share our space with each other and because of our willingness to extend grace to each other when needed, so that we can always experience the grace of God as a couple. We believe that these principles will also help your marriage climb to bigger and better heights as well!

The older we become, the more we appreciate the space and grace we give each other.

Take Away

This book has been about giving space and grace so that you can have a bigger and better marriage, the kind of marriage God's wants for you. While books, including this one, can give you tips, suggestions, examples, and the benefit of our experience, no book can substitute for you having a relationship with God. God alone is the foundation of a bigger and better marriage because he is the biggest and the best.

When we can't find it within ourselves to give our partners space and grace, God is able and willing to give space and grace to us so we can share it with others. In fact, the more we share grace and space, the more we will have.

As Vanessa and I close this chapter, we hope this book will aid and assist you in opening a new chapter in your marriage. We would like to pray two prayers with you and your family. Even though we didn't write these prayers, they still pack power.

We were taught these prayers by my father and Vanessa's mother. We combined the prayers to provide a hedge of protection around us, and it will do the same for you.

God grant unto us the serenity to except those things that we cannot change, the power to change those that we can, and the wisdom to know the difference. Now may the grace of our God and the sweet communion of his Holy Spirit rest, rule, and abide with you henceforth now and forever. Amen!

Offering Space and Grace

1. What are your plans for retirement? What are you looking forward to? What worries you about growing older?

2. Share a family story that you want to share with your grandchildren. What are three things you want your grandchildren to know about you?

3. Discuss how or if you have changed since you were a young adult. How are you better? What would you still like to learn and do?

4. What are some things that you plan to do differently with your grandchildren than you did with your children?

5. As you look back over this study, what stands out to you? Are there changes or adjustments you plan to make? If so, make a list and a time line to make them happen.

6. What are five things that you've learned about yourself and your spouse during this study?

Endorsements

If you want your marriage to grow to the next level, then this book is for you. Bishop Stephen and Co-Pastor Vanessa Hall are passionate about helping couples achieve the best results for a loving and healthy marriage. *Space and Grace to Build a Bigger and Better Marriage* is not just a book to read, however, it is a practical guide that will help enrich your marriage and help you live in matrimonial harmony with your spouse.

Bishop Paul S.Morton, Sr.
Founder, Full Gospel Baptist Church Fellowship International
Senior Pastor, Changing a Generation Ministries, Atlanta, Georgia
Overseer and Co-Pastor, Greater St. Stephen Ministries, New Orleans, Louisiana

Stephen and Vanessa Hall have set a very high bar. On one hand, they have this truly incredible marriage. On the other hand, they know what it takes to have sustainability, productivity, and collaboration. This wonderful read is a work from the heart. I know you will want to share it and use it as a tool in your church, book club, recommended reading, or personal devotion. I highly recommend it!

Dr. Brian Keith Hodges,
Pastor, Leadership Coach, Consultant

Marriage is one of the first institutions created and held in high esteem by God. In fact, the divine precedent for family union is apparent from the earliest pages in Scripture. In Genesis, Eve is created from Adam's side, and the covenant partnership intended between man and woman ensues. God so adamantly approved of the union that He "blessed them" (Genesis 1:28) and called their union "good" (Genesis 1:31). From the opening pages of the Bible, God shows us His endorsement of the marriage union.

Yet, one undeniable fact is that the institution of marriage has also suffered from an aggressive assault waged by the enemy, Satan. Each day, we encounter new and subtle attacks that seek to undermine the biblical foundations of marriage and weaken God's institution for family life. Because of this, we applaud Bishop Stephen B. Hall for providing an outstanding biblical resource to help strengthen marriages. This book, *Grace and Space to Build a Bigger and Better Marriage*, will not only help us understand why godly marriage works, but it will also help us in our assignment to support biblical marriage as the best foundation for successful families.

Dr. Craig L. Oliver, Sr.
Pastor, Elizabeth Baptist Church

At the close of the Creation project, God established two sacred institutions: sabbath and marriage. Sabbath was the context that man and woman would rest from work to focus their affections toward God. Marriage was the holy, inseparable union through which man and woman would focus their love and lives toward each other. In this, we must be reminded that marriage was God's idea, not ours; and thus marriage is a perfect institution derived from the perfect mind of a perfect God. Yet herein lies our challenge: How do imperfect individuals co-exist in a perfect institution? The 'elephant-in-the-room' for married couples continues to be: How do I be me and be yours at the same time?

Bishop Stephen Hall and Co-Pastor Vanessa Hall have written this book to provide further resolution to the challenges that oppose marriage, as well as their advocacy of God's intended bliss through marriage. This book will empower husbands and wives to live holy, happy, and healthy marriages. It does us all well to welcome this fresh perspective from a priestly couple so we can all experience the space and grace of a better marriage.

Tolan J. Morgan, Sr.
Pastor, Fellowship Bible Baptist Church

The three most important decisions that people can make are what will be their master, who will be their mate, and how they will make their money. Many people will say that the most difficult of the aforementioned choices is the second one. Determining the person to take wedding vows has become a major issue for men and women of all races, religions, and economic status. The majority of the problems generally surface after the honeymoon period is over.

As a result of this, married couples can greatly benefit from resources that will help them survive and thrive as husbands and wives. A great tool that is available is Bishop Stephen and Lady Vanessa Hall's book, *Space and Grace to Build a Bigger and Better Marriage*.

In this book, the Halls address the challenges and triumphs of sharing life and space with another. Throughout the pages of *Space and Grace,* you discover what it takes to blend and grow in marriage. Use this very valuable resource to help you before and during marriage.

Dr. Kerwin Lee, Sr.
Pastor, Berean Christian Church

9 780692 722367